D1147014

646.42
NOR

7 DAY
BOOK

beauty basics

WITHDRAWN

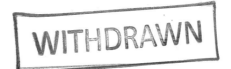
COLEG GLAN HAFREN LRC PARADE

Habia SERIES – RELATED TITLES

HAIRDRESSING

Student textbooks

Begin Hairdressing: The Official Guide to Level 1 1e *Martin Green*

Hairdressing – The Foundations: The Official Guide to Level 2 5e *Leo Palladino and Martin Green*

Professional Hairdressing: The Official Guide to Level 3 5e *Leo Palladino and Martin Green*

The Official Guide to the City & Guilds Certificate in Salon Services 1e *John Armstrong with Anita Crosland, Martin Green and Lorraine Nordmann*

The Colour Book: The Official Guide to Colour for NVQ Levels 2 & 3 1e *Tracey Lloyd with Christine McMillan-Bodell*

eXtensions: The Official Guide to Hair Extensions 1e *Theresa Bullock*

Salon Management 1e *Martin Green*

Men's Hairdressing: Traditional and Modern Barbering 2e *Maurice Lister*

African-Caribbean Hairdressing 2e *Sandra Gittens*

The World of Hair Colour 1e *Dr John Gray*

Professional Hairdressing titles

Trevor Sorbie: The Bridal Hair Book 1e *Trevor Sorbie and Jacki Wadeson*

The Art of Dressing Long Hair 1e *Guy Kremer and Jacki Wadeson*

Patrick Cameron: Dressing Long Hair 1e *Patrick Cameron and Jacki Wadeson*

Patrick Cameron: Dressing Long Hair 2 1e *Patrick Cameron and Jacki Wadeson*

Bridal Hair 1e *Pat Dixon and Jacki Wadeson*

Professional Men's Hairdressing: The Art of Cutting and Styling 1e *Guy Kremer and Jacki Wadeson*

Essensuals, the Next Generation Toni and Guy: Step by Step 1e *Sacha Mascolo, Christian Mascolo and Stuart Wesson*

Mahogany Hairdressing: Steps to Cutting, Colouring and Finishing Hair 1e *Martin Gannon and Richard Thompson*

Mahogany Hairdressing: Advanced Looks 1e *Martin Gannon and Richard Thompson*

The Total Look: The Style Guide for Hair and Make-Up Professionals 1e *Ian Mistlin*

Trevor Sorbie: Visions in Hair 1e *Trevor Sorbie, Kris Sorbie and Jacki Wadeson*

The Art of Hair Colouring 1e *David Adams and Jacki Wadeson*

BEAUTY THERAPY

Beauty Basics: The Official Guide to Level 1 2e *Lorraine Nordmann*

Beauty Therapy – The Foundations: The Official Guide to Level 2 4e *Lorraine Nordmann*

Professional Beauty Therapy: The Official Guide to Level 3 3e *Lorraine Nordmann*

The Official Guide to the City & Guilds Certificate in Salon Services 1e *John Armstrong with Anita Crosland, Martin Green and Lorraine Nordmann*

Encyclopedia of Hair Removal 1e *Gill Morris and Janice Brown*

The Complete Guide to Make-Up 1e *Suzanne Le Quesne*

The Complete Make-Up Artist 2e *Penny Delamar*

The Encyclopedia of Nails 2e *Jacqui Jefford and Anne Swain*

The Art of Nails: A Comprehensive Style Guide to Nail Treatments and Nail Art 1e *Jacqui Jefford*

Nail Artistry 1e *Jacqui Jefford, Sue Marsh and Anne Swain*

The Complete Nail Technician 2e *Marian Newman*

Manicure, Pedicure and Advanced Nail Techniques 1e *Elaine Almond*

The Official Guide to Body Massage 2e *Adele O'Keefe*

An Holistic Guide to Massage 1e *Tina Parsons*

Indian Head Massage 2e *Muriel Burnham-Airey and Adele O'Keefe*

Aromatherpy for the Beauty Therapist 1e *Valerie Ann Worwood*

An Holistic Guide to Reflexology 1e *Tina Parsons*

An Holistic Guide to Anatomy and Physiology 1e *Tina Parsons*

The Essential Guide to Holistic and Complementary Therapy 1e *Helen Beckmann and Suzanne Le Quesne*

The Spa Book 1e *Jane Crebbin-Bailey, Dr John Harcup and John Harrington*

Nutrition: A Practical Approach 1e *Suzanne Le Quesne*

Hands on Sports Therapy 1e *Keith Ward*

beauty basics

THE OFFICIAL GUIDE TO LEVEL 1

SECOND EDITION

LORRAINE NORDMANN

habia
standards · information · solutions

City&
Guilds

THOMSON

Australia • Canada • Mexico • Singapore • Spain • United Kingdom • United States

Beauty Basics, Second Edition
Lorraine Nordmann

Publishing Director
John Yates

Commissioning Editor
Melody Dawes

Development Editors
Lizzie Catford
Emily Gibson

Production Editor
Emily Gibson

Manufacturing Manager
Helen Mason

Marketing Manager
Leo Stanley

Typesetter
Meridian Colour Repro Ltd., Berkshire

Production Controller
Maeve Healy

Illustrations
Oxford Designers and Illustrators

Text Design
Design Deluxe Ltd., Bath, UK

Cover Design
Jackie Wrout, Land-Sky Ltd

Printer
Canale, Italy

Copyright © 2007
Thomson Learning

The Thomson logo is a registered trademark used herein under licence.

For more information, contact
Thomson Learning
High Holborn House
50-51 Bedford Row
London WC1R 4LR

or visit us on the World Wide Web at:
http://www.thomsonlearning.co.uk

ISBN: 978-1-84480-694-2

First edition published 2005 by
Thomson Learning

This edition published 2007 by Thomson Learning. All rights reserved by Thomson Learning 2007. The text of this publication, or any part thereof, may not be reproduced or transmitted in any form or by any means, electronic or mechanical, including photocopying, recording, storage in an information retrieval system, or otherwise, without prior permission of the publisher.

Every effort has been made to trace all the copyright holders, but if any have been inadvertently overlooked the publisher will be pleased to make the necessary arrangements at the first opportunity. Please contact the publisher directly.

While the publisher has taken all reasonable care in the preparation of this book the publisher makes no representation, express or implied, with regard to the accuracy of the information contained in this book and cannot accept any legal responsibility or liability for any errors or omissions from the book or the consequences thereof.

Products and services that are referred to in this book may be either trademarks and/or registered trademarks of their respective owners. The publisher and author/s make no claim to these trademarks.

British Library Cataloguing-in-Publication Data
A catalogue record for this book is available from the British Library

This publication has been developed by Thomson Learning. It is intended as a method of studying for the Habia qualifications. Thomson Learning has taken all reasonable care in the preparation of this publication but Thomson Learning and the City and Guilds of London Institute accept no liability howsoever in respect of any breach of the rights of any third party howsoever occasioned or damage caused to any third party as a result of the use of this publication.

contents

foreword

It is a pleasure for me to write this foreword for *Beauty Basics*, which completes the pioneering trilogy of beauty therapy texts by Lorraine Nordmann.

Originally written to accompany a significant and exciting change within the industry – the introduction of the Level 1 beauty therapy qualification – for me, there was no question of who would write this text for the Habia and Thomson Learning partnership.

Since then, the beauty industry has grown from strength to strength, advancing in professionalism, technology and capability. UK standards are widely considered the best in the world and I am certain that Lorraine has played a huge role in pushing the development of beauty to the quality we now see. The release of this second edition of *Beauty Basics* is testament to that.

An inspirational educationalist and practitioner, Lorraine has an abundance of industry knowledge and experience. She radiates professional aura, a result of her enthusiasm and passion for developing original learning materials for beauty therapists of all levels.

As you start your qualification and begin your career in a world full of opportunities, take Lorraine Nordmann's dedication and motivation as inspiration that great success can be achieved.

Alan Goldsbro
Chief Executive Officer, Habia

introduction

AN INTRODUCTION TO NVQS/SVQS

National Vocational Qualifications (NVQs) and Scottish Vocational Qualifications (SVQs) are nationally recognised qualifications and have a common structure and design. They follow a similar format for all occupational and vocational sectors. The award of an NVQ/SVQ demonstrates that the person has the competence (i.e. sufficient skill and knowledge) to perform job roles/tasks effectively in their occupational area.

An NVQ/SVQ at Level 1 covers mainly routine work activities. In beauty therapy these include preparing and maintaining the work area and assisting others in their work roles. Your actions are important and will ensure the smooth running of the salon activities, reduce risks to health and safety and improve the quality of the service offered to clients.

Each NVQ/SVQ is structured the same way, and is made up of a number of units and outcomes:

- The term **unit** relates to a specific task or skill area of work. It is the smallest part of the award that can be accredited separately.
- The **outcome(s)** describes in further detail the skill and knowledge requirements for each unit.

An example from NVQ Level 1 Beauty Therapy is given below:

- The title of the unit is **Unit BT2: Assist with facial treatments**.
- The outcomes for the unit detail the practical skills and underpinning knowledge essential to assist with facial treatments. The outcomes that detail the unit components include:

Units and outcomes

For each unit, when all competence requirements have been achieved, a unit of certification can be awarded, such as **Unit BT2: Assist with facial treatments**.

Each NVQ/SVQ is made up of a specific number of units required for the occupational area. For NVQ/SVQ Level 1 Beauty Therapy, all the units are termed **mandatory units** (compulsory) and each must be competently achieved to gain the NVQ/SVQ award.

The following mandatory units make up the Beauty Therapy NVQ/SVQ qualification in **Beauty Therapy at Level 1** (all must be completed):

- G1: Ensure your own actions reduce risks to health and safety
- G2: Assist with salon reception duties
- BT1: Prepare and maintain the beauty therapy work area
- BT2: Assist with facial treatments
- BT3: Assist with nail treatments on the hands.

Performance criteria

The performance criteria list the necessary actions you must achieve to complete the task competently (demonstrating adequate practical skill and experience to the assessor). For example, the **performance criteria** requirements for Unit BT2, Outcome 2: Carry out facial treatments (each stage of the facial treatment) are listed below:

a maintain hygiene and safety throughout the treatment

b using facial products correctly and following manufacturers' instructions

c using suitable techniques to deep cleanse the client's skin

d checking that the skin is left clean and free from all traces of make-up

e applying pre-prepared non-setting mask treatments evenly and neatly, ensuring that the area to be treated is covered

f removing masks after the recommended time and without discomfort to the client

g applying the correct toner and moisturiser

h ensuring that the skin is left clean, toned and suitably moisturised.

Range

Range statements are often identified for the different elements. The assessment range relates to the different conditions under which a skill must be demonstrated competently to pass the outcome. For example, the **range** assessment requirements for Unit BT2, Outcome 2 below lists the skin types to be covered:

Range Your performance must cover the following situations

Skin types are:
  a oily
  b dry
  c combination

It is not sufficient to be able to perform the task practically, you must **understand** why you are doing it and be able to transfer your competence to a variety of situations. This is called **knowledge and understanding**. Further assessment of your knowledge and understanding of the skill, the knowledge specification, is made through theoretical tasks such as written tests, assignments and oral questioning.

The **knowledge and understanding** requirements required for **Unit BT2: Facial treatments** are listed below:

- the different cleansing techniques used within facial treatments and how to carry them out
- the reasons for cleansing, toning, mask application and moisturising
- the benefits of cleansing, toning, mask application and moisturising.

It is often the case that the same knowledge and understanding is necessary for similar units. This can be seen, for example, in the knowledge and understanding for **Organisational and Legal Requirements**.

Where evidence has been achieved this is cross-referenced (directed) in the portfolio (a file that holds your assessment evidence) in which the evidence can be found.

To achieve unit competence, all performance criteria, range and knowledge and understanding requirements must have been met and the necessary evidence presented. Evidence is usually provided in your assessment book and portfolio.

Beauty Basics – The Official Guide to Level 1 follows the Beauty Therapy NVQ/SVQ Level 1 format and covers both the practical and theoretical requirements for each mandatory unit. On successful completion of Level 1 Beauty Therapy you can progress and study towards an NVQ/SVQ Level 2 in Beauty Therapy.

You will then find all the practical and theoretical requirements for your new programme of study in *Beauty Therapy: The Foundations – The Official Guide to Level 2* (Thomson Learning, 2007).

ABOUT THIS BOOK

The book relates to the NVQ/SVQ Level 1, five-unit qualification structure and has five chapters each related to a specific NVQ/SVQ unit.

Features within chapters

Common features appear in the chapters, and an explanation of each is provided below:

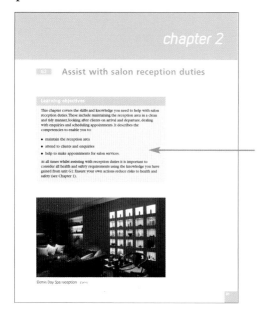

Learning objectives

All the chapters are introduced by the **learning objectives** section, which lists the outcomes that make up the unit and which must be achieved in order to be accredited with the NVQ/SVQ unit. When you feel confident and competent with the skills/knowledge requirements you are ready to be assessed.

Unit outcomes

Unit outcomes are provided in each chapter to summarise the skills/knowledge requirement for each outcome. These provide a useful checklist.

Practical skills and knowledge checklist

The **practical skills and knowledge checklist** at the beginning of each chapter breaks down each stage of the treatment service. These are provided for each unit. When you feel you have the necessary skills and knowledge in each area you can ask your assessor to assess you on the unit.

Health and safety boxes

In addition to Chapter 1, **Unit G1: Ensure your own actions reduce risks to health and safety**, health and safety boxes are provided in each chapter. They serve to draw your attention to related health and safety information for each technical skill.

Use of bold terms

The text highlights certain terms set in **bold** lettering. This information is often important or a technical term that you must become familiar with to gain knowledge competence for the unit.

Tip boxes

The author's experience is shared through **tip boxes**, which provide positive suggestions to improve your knowledge and skills for each unit.

Activity boxes

Activity boxes feature within the chapters and provide additional tasks for you to complete to assess and further your understanding of the unit content.

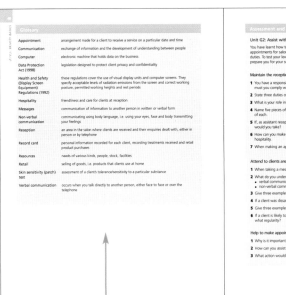

In addition to the activity boxes in each chapter, questions are provided at the end of each chapter. These questions relate to the specific **essential knowledge and understanding requirements** for the unit. You can use the questions to prepare you for oral and written assessments. Seek guidance from your supervisor/assessor if there are any areas that you are unsure of.

Glossary

A list of technical words, relevant legislation and their meanings is provided in the **glossary** at the end of each chapter. This also provides a useful checklist to test your understanding.

Step-by-step photo sequences

Those chapters demonstrating a practical skill requirement contain **step-by-step** colour images to enhance your understanding.

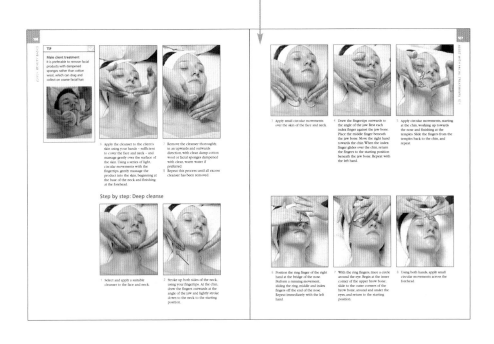

Treatment record cards

Sample **client treatment record cards** are featured. You are responsible for obtaining these before treatment and for storing them securely after treatment. These cards contain information that will be needed to establish client suitability and treatment aims; this information will be gained from the client at the consultation. The cards also record what information was provided after treatment, including aftercare advice and the promotion of additional products and services.

Equipment, material and products checklists

To help you prepare for each practical treatment, an **essential equipment list** is provided, supported with images of treatment tools, materials and products required. These are particularly useful when you are assisting to prepare the work area for Level 2 treatments.

Anatomy and physiology

Certain units have an **anatomy and physiology** knowledge requirement. The specific anatomy and physiology requirements for these units is discussed fully within the relevant chapters, without the need to refer elsewhere.

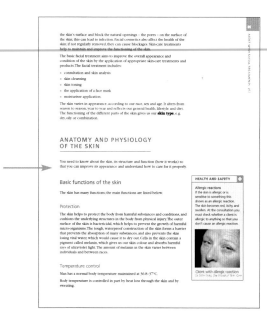

about the author

Lorraine Nordmann has over twenty years of experience in the beauty therapy industry – an industry she has seen grow significantly in status, technology and specialisms during her roles as lecturer, assessor and external verifier for City and Guilds. She aims to ensure that this high profile of the beauty therapy industry is maintained.

Lorraine is also the author of the Habia official guides *Beauty Therapy – The Foundations* and *Professional Beauty Therapy*, covering the latest industry standards at NVQ/SQV Levels 2 and 3.

acknowledgements

The authors and publishers would like to thank the following for their help with providing images for the book:

Beauty Express
Dr. M. H. Beck
Richard Corfield
Creative Nail Design
Adam Birtwistle at Sorisa
Diane Burkhill at Depilex/RVB
Ez Flow
Judith Ford
Chubb Fire Ltd.
Derma Colour
Dream Workwear
Dr. John Gray, *The World of Skin Care*
Habia, the Hair and Beauty Industry Authority
The Health and Safety Executive
HMSO
Moom
IBD
Jessica Nails
Salon Systems
Clean + Easy
Elemis Ltd.
Millennium Nails
Oxford Designers and Illustrators
Emma Kenny and Pam Linforth at Ellisons
Hugh Rushton
John Birtwistle at Silhouette-Dermalift
Smith and Nephew, Hull
Sally Smith at Original Additions Ltd
Nicole Warwick at Designer Nails UK Ltd
Caroline Morley at the Wellcome Photo Library
Dr. A. L. Wright
8.1.9.18 Divas, Uckfield

Every effort has been made to trace all copyright holders but, if any have been inadvertently overlooked, the publishers will be pleased to make any necessary arrangements at the first opportunity.

chapter 1

G1 Ensure your own actions reduce risks to health and safety

Learning objectives

This chapter covers health and safety duties and responsibilities for everyone in the workplace. It is important that your own actions do not create any health and safety risks; that you do not ignore significant risks or hazards in your workplace; and you take sensible action to put things right, including reporting situations that pose a danger to people in the workplace and seeking advice where necessary. It describes the competencies required to ensure that you:

- identify the hazards and evaluate the risks in your workplace
- reduce the risks to health and safety in your workplace.

Everyone is responsible for health and safety   Depilex/RVB

PRACTICAL SKILLS AND KNOWLEDGE

This table will help you to check your progress in gaining the necessary practical skills and knowledge for Unit G1: Ensure your own actions reduce risks to health and safety.

Tick (✓), when you feel you have gained your practical skills and knowledge in the following areas:

Practical skills and knowledge checklist	✓
1 The correct environmental conditions for each treatment, including: ● lighting ● heating ● ventilation ● general client comfort	
2 Preventing infection – selecting and using the correct method of disinfection/sterilisation for tools, equipment and general salon hygiene	
3 Taking care of yourself, clients and colleagues following all health and safety requirements	
4 Wearing protective, hygienic clothing and maintaining a professional appearance	
5 Carrying out services in accordance with legal requirements and workplace policy	
6 Following the correct waste removal and disposal systems	
7 Knowing who to refer to for guidance on issues relating to health and safety in the workplace	
8 Avoiding potential hazards and risks within your job role, through safe working practices and personal conduct	
9 Knowing when to pass on information immediately, reporting potential risks or hazards to the relevant person	
10 Dealing with low-risk hazards within your responsibility, following workplace policy and legal requirements	
11 Following manufacturers' guidelines for the care and maintenance of equipment and product use and storage	
12 Knowing who to notify and the procedure to follow in the event of an accident or emergency	
13 Knowing the correct fire safety procedure to follow in the event of a fire	

HEALTH AND SAFETY

Health and Safety Executive
The Health and Safety Executive (HSE) ensures that health and safety laws are being followed. Two important aspects – hazards and risks – will be minimised if an effective workplace health and safety policy is followed:
Hazard: something with the potential to cause harm
Risk: the likelihood of a hazard's potential being realised.
It is important that hazards do not become risks.

When you have ticked all the areas, you can ask your assessor to assess you on Unit G1: Ensure your own actions reduce risks to health and safety. After practical assessment, your assessor might decide that you need to practise further to improve your skills. If so, your assessor will tell you how and where you need to improve to gain competence.

HEALTH AND SAFETY IN THE WORKPLACE

When working in the beauty therapy industry, you are legally obliged to provide a **safe and hygienic environment**. You must pay careful attention to health and safety practice to minimise risk.

Outcome: Identify and reduce hazards and risks in your workplace

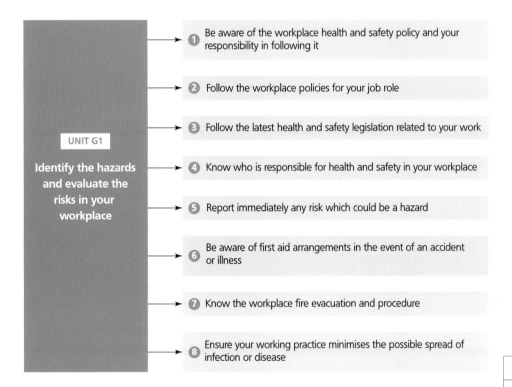

UNIT G1

Identify the hazards and evaluate the risks in your workplace

1 Be aware of the workplace health and safety policy and your responsibility in following it

2 Follow the workplace policies for your job role

3 Follow the latest health and safety legislation related to your work

4 Know who is responsible for health and safety in your workplace

5 Report immediately any risk which could be a hazard

6 Be aware of first aid arrangements in the event of an accident or illness

7 Know the workplace fire evacuation and procedure

8 Ensure your working practice minimises the possible spread of infection or disease

Legal responsibilities

If you cause harm to your client, or put a client at risk, you will be held responsible and you will be liable to **prosecution**, with the possibility of being fined.

There is a good deal of **legislation** relating to health and safety. Details are widely available and you must be aware of your responsibilities and your rights. It is important that you obtain and read all relevant publications.

ACTIVITY

Keep up to date
Health and safety information is continually being updated. Write to your local Health and Safety Executive (HSE) office and ask for a pack of relevant health and safety information or visit their websides:
www.hse.go.uk and
www.hsedirect.gov.uk.

ACTIVITY

Health and safety rules
Discuss the rules which apply to you in your salon's health and safety policy. The health and safety policy identifies how health and safety is managed: who does what, when and why.

HEALTH AND SAFETY

Health and safety notice
Every employer is obliged by law to display a health and safety notice in the workplace. This is required by the legislation Health and Safety (Information for Employees) Regulations 1989.

HEALTH AND SAFETY

Gloves
You should wear protective disposable surgical gloves if you are likely to come into contact with body tissue fluids or with chemicals. This is called Personal Protective Equipment (PPE).

ACTIVITY

PPE Risk assessment
Carry out your own risk assessment. List the potentially hazardous substances that you may be required to handle. What protective clothing should be available?

The Health and Safety at Work Act (1974)

This Act developed from experience gained over 150 years and incorporates earlier legislation, including the Offices, Shops and Railway Premises Act (1963) and the Fire Precautions Act (1971). It lays down the minimum standards of health, safety and welfare required in each area of the workplace. For example, it requires business premises and equipment to be safe and in good repair. It is the employer's responsibility to implement the Act and to ensure that the workplace is safe both for employees and for clients.

All employers of more than five employees must have a written **health and safety policy** for that establishment. The policy must be issued to every employee and should outline their safety responsibilities. It should include items such as:

- details of the storage of chemical substances
- details of the stock cupboard or dispensary
- details and records of the checks made by a qualified electrician on specialist electrical equipment
- names and addresses of the person(s) with a key to the premises (the key holders)
- escape routes and emergency evacuation procedures
- rules on working practices
- personal presentation and hygiene
- rules on eating and drinking and drug use.

Regular checks should be made to ensure that safety is being satisfactorily maintained.

Employees must co-operate with their employer to provide a safe and healthy workplace. As soon as an employee observes a **hazard** this must be reported to the designated authority so that the problem can be put right. Hazards include:

- obstructions to corridors, stairways and fire exits
- spillages and breakages.

An obstruction occurs when an object blocks a traffic route or exit, creating a hazard. Obstructions are dangerous because they can cause accidents but also, in the event of an emergency such as a fire, an obstruction could prove fatal. Removing an obstruction is an example of avoiding potential hazards and risks in the workplace.

In 1992, European Union (EU) directives updated the legislation on health and safety management. Current legislation (at the time of writing – 2007) is outlined below.

The Management of Health and Safety at Work Regulations (1999)

These require employers to make formal arrangements for maintaining and improving safe working conditions and practices. This includes training for employees and the monitoring of risk in the workplace, known as **risk assessment**.

The Personal Protective Equipment (PPE) at Work Regulations (1992)

These require managers to identify – through a **risk assessment** – activities or processes that require special protective clothing or equipment to be worn. This clothing and equipment must then be made available, in adequate supplies. Employees must wear the protective clothing and use the protective equipment provided, and should make employers aware of any shortage so that supplies can be maintained.

TIP

Unpacking
When you unpack a delivery, make sure the product packaging is undamaged. Damaged products may be hazardous, for example, broken glass or spilt chemicals.

The Workplace (Health, Safety and Welfare) Regulations (1992)

These require everyone at work to maintain a safe, healthy and secure working environment. The regulations include legal requirements in relation to the following aspects of the working environment:

- maintenance of the workplace and equipment
- ventilation
- working temperature
- lighting
- cleanliness and handling of waste materials
- safe salon layout
- falls and falling objects
- windows, doors, gates and walls
- safe floor and traffic routes
- escalators and moving walkways
- sanitary conveniences
- washing facilities
- drinking water
- facilities for changing clothing
- facilities for staff to rest and eat meals
- fire exits and firefighting equipment.

ACTIVITY

Health and safety: European directives
As a result of directives adopted in 1992 by the European Union, health and safety legislation has been updated.
1 Obtain a copy of the new directives. Workplace (Health & Safety & Welfare) Regulations 1992.
2 Look through the publication, and make notes on any information relevant to you in the workplace.

Manual Handling Operations Regulations (1992)

These regulations apply in all occupations that require manual lifting. The employer is required to carry out a risk assessment of all activities that involve manual lifting. The risk assessment should provide evidence that the following have been considered:

- risk of injury
- the manual movement involved in performing the activity
- the physical force the load requires in order to move it
- the environmental constraints imposed by the workplace
- workers' individual capabilities
- action taken to minimise potential risks.

TIP

Salon temperature
The salon temperature should be a minimum of 16°C within one hour of employees arriving for work. The salon should be well ventilated, or carbon dioxide levels will increase, which can cause nausea. Many substances used in the salon can become hazardous without adequate ventilation.
If the working environment is too warm this can cause heat stress, a condition that is recognised by the HSE.
Lighting should be adequate to ensure that treatments can be carried out safely and competently, with the minimum risk of accident.

HEALTH AND SAFETY: MANUAL LIFTING AND HANDLING ✚

Always take care of yourself when moving goods around the salon. Do not struggle or be impatient: get someone else to help. When **lifting**, lift from the knees, not the back. When **carrying**, balance weights evenly in both hands and carry the heaviest part nearest to your body.

Lifting a box   Carrying several boxes   Carrying equal weights in both hands

HEALTH AND SAFETY ✚

Health and Safety Training
Training in equipment use.
As a level 1 beauty therapist you will be required to prepare the work area for level 2 treatments. This will involve sometimes electrical equipment, i.e. wax heaters. Make sure you have had training in how these should be prepared safely for use.

Correctly seated computer operator
HMSO

Provision and Use of Work Equipment Regulations (PUWER) (1998)

These regulations lay down the important health and safety controls on the provision and use of work equipment. They state the duties for employers and for users, including the self-employed. They affect both old and new equipment and identify the requirements for selecting suitable equipment and for maintaining it. They also discuss the information provided by equipment manufacturers, and the instruction and training in the safe use of equipment. Specific regulations cover the dangers and potential risks of injury that could occur during use of the equipment.

Health and Safety (Display Screen Equipment) (1992)

These regulations cover the use of visual display units (VDUs) and computer screens. They specify acceptable levels of radiation emissions from the screen and identify correct posture, seating position, permitted working heights and rest periods.

Control of Substances Hazardous to Health (COSHH) Regulations (2002)

These regulations were designed to make employers consider the substances used in their workplace and assess the possible risks to health. Many substances that seem quite harmless can prove to be hazardous if used or stored incorrectly. Hazardous substances are anything that can harm your health.

Employers are responsible for assessing the risks from hazardous substances and controlling exposure to them to prevent ill health. Any hazardous substances identified must be formally recorded in writing and given a hazard risk rating. Safety procedures should then be implemented and employees trained to ensure that the procedures are understood and will be followed correctly.

Hazardous substances are identified by the use of symbols. Any substance in the workplace that is hazardous to health must be identified on the packaging and stored and handled correctly.

Hazardous substances can enter the body via the:

- eyes
- skin
- nose (inhalation)
- mouth (ingestion).

All beauty product suppliers are legally required to produce guidelines on how materials should be used and stored. These are called material safety data sheets (MSDSs) and the manufacturer must supply these on request.

Cosmetic Products (Safety) Regulations 2004

This piece of legislation consolidates earlier regulations and incorporates current European directives. Part of consumer protective legislation, it requires that cosmetics and toiletries are safe and comply with labelling requirements.

Electricity at Work Regulations (1989)

These regulations state that every piece of electrical equipment in the workplace must be tested every 12 months by a qualified electrician. In addition to annual testing, a trained member of staff should check all electrical equipment for safety; this should occur every three months. Report to your supervisor if you see any of these potential hazards:

- exposed wires in flexes
- cracked plugs or broken sockets
- worn cables
- overloaded sockets.

Although it is the employer's responsibility to ensure that all equipment is safe to use, it is also the responsibility of the employee to check that equipment is safe before use, and never to use faulty equipment.

Any pieces of equipment that appear faulty must be checked immediately and repaired (if faulty) before use. If faulty and unrepaired, they must be labelled so that they are not used by accident.

Accidents

Accidents in the workplace are usually the result of negligence by employees or unsafe working conditions. Any accidents occurring the workplace must be recorded on a **report form** and entered into an **accident book**. The report form requires more details than the accident book. You must note:

- the date and time of the accident
- the date of entry into the accident book

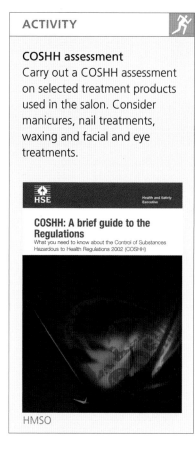

ACTIVITY

COSHH assessment
Carry out a COSHH assessment on selected treatment products used in the salon. Consider manicures, nail treatments, waxing and facial and eye treatments.

COSHH: A brief guide to the Regulations
What you need to know about the Control of Substances Hazardous to Health Regulations 2002 (COSHH)

HMSO

TIP

A COSHH essential information document is available at www.coshh-essentials.org.uk. HSE publication ISBN 0717627853 gives guidance on COSHH assessment

Six hazard symbols

ACTIVITY

Identifying hazards
Make a list of potential electrical hazards in the workplace, e.g. damaged plugs. Who should these be reported to?

HEALTH AND SAFETY +

Appoint a responsible person
It is useful to appoint a person to be responsible for maintaining the first aid equipment and for seeking assistance (if required) if there is not a designated first aider. Who is you first aider?

ACTIVITY

Avoiding accidents
Discuss potential causes of accidents in the workplace. How could these accidents be prevented?

- the name of the person or people involved
- details of the accident
- details of the injuries caused as a result of the accident
- the action taken
- the signature of the person making the entry.

ACCIDENT REPORT FORM

date and time of accident: . . . .   location of accident: . . . .

address: . . . .

postcode: . . . .   telephone number: . . . .

name of injured person: . . . .   address: . . . .

postcode: . . . .   telephone number: . . . .

INJURIES

part(s) of the body affected: . . . .   nature of injuries: . . . .

how did the accident happen: . . . .

first aid given, record details: . . . .   name of first aider: . . . .

WITNESSES

name(s): . . . .   address: . . . .

postcode: . . . .   telephone number: . . . .

details recorded in the accident record book? . . . . .

signature of injured person: . . . .   signature of first aider: . . . .

signature of witness: . . . .   signature of witness: . . . .

signature of supervisor: . . . .

An accident report form

HEALTH AND SAFETY

Breakages and Spillages
Accidents can damage stock, resulting in breakage of containers and spillage of contents. Breakage of glass can cause cuts; spillages can cause somebody to slip and fall. Any breakages or spillages should therefore be dealt with immediately and in the correct way. When dealing with hazardous breakages and spillages, the hands should always be protected with gloves. To avoid injury to others, broken glass should be put in a secure container prior to disposing of it in a waste bin. You must determine whether the spillage is a potential hazard to health and what action is necessary. To whom should you report it? What equipment is required to remove the spillage? How should the materials be disposed of?
Always remember COSHH and check to see how the product should be handled and disposed of.

Reporting of Injuries, Diseases and Dangerous Occurrences Regulations (RIDDOR) (1995)

These require the employer to notify the local enforcement officer, in writing, when employees suffer personal injury at work. If this results in death, major injury or more than 24 hours in hospital, it must be reported by telephone first and followed by a written report within 7 days. In all cases of personal injury, an entry must be made in the workplace accident book. The information helps the Health and Safety Executive to investigate serious accidents.

Disposal of waste

Waste should be disposed of in an enclosed waste bin fitted with a polythene bin liner that is durable enough not to tear. The bin should be disinfected regularly in a well-ventilated area: wear protective gloves when doing this. Hazardous waste must be disposed of following the COSHH procedures and employees should be trained in these.

Clinical (contaminated) waste is waste derived from human tissues. This includes blood and tissue fluids such as wax strips and should be disposed of as recommended by the Environment Agency in accordance with the Controlled Waste Regulations 1992. Items that have been used to pierce the skin, such as disposable milia extractors, should be discarded in a disposable **sharps container**. Again, contact your local environment health department to check on disposal arrangements.

Inspection and registration of premises

Inspectors from the HSE or your local authority enforce health and safety law. They visit the workplace to ensure compliance with government legislation is being met. If the officer identifies an area of danger an **improvement notice** will be issued and it is the employer's responsibility to remove the danger within a designated period of time. Failure to comply with the notice will lead to prosecution. The inspector also has the authority to close a business until they are satisfied that all danger to employees and public has been removed. Such closure involves issuing a **prohibition notice**.

Certain treatments carried out in beauty therapy, such as ear piercing, pose additional risk because they might produce blood and body tissue fluid. Inspection of the premises is necessary before such services can be offered to the public. The inspector will visit to make sure that the guidelines listed in the **Local Government (Miscellaneous Provisions) Act (1982)** relating to this area are being complied with. When the inspector is satisfied, a certificate of registration will be awarded.

First aid

Health and Safety (First Aid) Regulations (1981)

The **Health and Safety (First Aid) Regulations (1981)** state that employers must have appropriate and adequate first aid arrangements in the event of an accident or illness.

All employees must be told of the first aid procedures, including:

- where to find the first aid box
- who is responsible for maintaining the first aid box
- which member of staff to inform in the event of an accident or illness occurring
- which staff member to inform in the event of an accident or emergency.

An adequately stocked first aid box should be available that complies with health and safety first aid requirements. As a minimum, this should contain:

First aid equipment
Smith and Nephew, Hull

- a basic first aid guidance leaflet (1)
- assorted sterile adhesive dressings (20)
- individually wrapped triangular bandages (6)
- safety pins (6)
- sterile eye pads, with attachments (2)
- medium-sized individually wrapped sterile unmedicated wound dressings 10 cm x 8 cm (6)
- large individually wrapped sterile unmedicated wound dressings 13 cm x 9 cm (2)
- extra large individually wrapped sterile unmedicated wound dressings 28 cm x 17.5 cm (3)
- individually wrapped medical wipes
- antiseptic cream or liquid
- sterile water in sealed containers to bathe the eyes, if tap water is not readily available.

> **TIP** ✓
>
> **First aid booklet**
> HSE guidance publication *First Aid* – ISBN 0717610705. This can be stored in the first aid box.

General guidance on first aid

Normally a casualty should be seated, or lying down, when being treated by a first aider.

Mouth-to-mouth resuscitation procedure

- Place the casualty on their back. Open and clear their mouth.
- Tilt head backwards to open airway (maintain this position throughout). Support the jaw.
- Kneel beside casualty, while keeping head backwards. Open mouth and pinch nose.
- Open your mouth and take a deep breath. Seal their mouth with yours and breathe firmly into it. Casualty's chest should rise. Remove your mouth and let their chest fall. If their chest does not rise, check their head is tilted sufficiently. Repeat at a rate of 10 times a minute until the casualty is breathing alone.
- Place them in the recovery position.

First aid procedures

Problem	Action to be taken
Casualty is not breathing	Use mouth-to-mouth resuscitation procedure.
Unconscious	Place into recovery position.
Severe bleeding	Control by direct pressure using fingers and thumb on the bleeding point. Apply a dressing. Raising the bleeding limb (unless it is broken) will reduce the flow of blood.
Suspected broken bones	Do not move the casualty unless they are in a position which exposes them to immediate danger.
Burns and scalds (due to heat)	Do not remove clothing sticking to the burns or scalds. Do not burst any blisters. If burns and scalds are small, flush them with plenty of clean, cool water before applying a sterilised dressing. If burns and scalds are large or deep, wash your hands, apply a dry sterilised dressing and send the casualty to hospital.
Burns (chemicals)	Avoid contaminating yourself with the chemical. Remove any contaminated clothing which is not stuck to skin. Flush with plenty of cool water for 10–15 minutes. Apply a sterilised dressing and send to hospital.
Foreign body in eye	Wash out eye with clean cool water. A person with an eye injury should be sent to hospital with the eye covered by an eye pad.
Chemicals in eyes	Wash out the open eye continuously with clean, cool water for 10–15 minutes.
Electric shock	Don't touch the casualty until the current is switched off. If the current cannot be switched off, stand on some dry insulating material and use a wooden or plastic implement to free the casualty from the electrical source. If breathing has stopped start mouth-to-mouth breathing and continue until the casualty starts to breathe by themselves or until professional help arrives.
Gassing	Use suitable protective equipment. Move casualty to fresh air. If breathing has stopped start mouth-to-mouth breathing and continue until the casualty is breathing themself or until professional help arrives. Send to hospital with a note of the gas involved.
Minor injuries	Casualties with minor injuries of a nature they would normally attend to themselves may wash their hands and apply a small sterilised dressing from the first aid box.

ACTIVITY

Fire drill
Each workplace should have a fire drill regularly. This enables staff to practise so that they know what to do in the event of a real fire. What is the fire drill procedure to your workplace?

Fire

The **Fire Precautions Act (1971)** states that all staff must be aware of and trained in fire and emergency evacuation procedures for their workplace. The **emergency exit route** will be the easiest route by which staff and clients can leave the building safely.

A **fire certificate** is a compulsory requirement of the Act if there are more than 20 employees, or if more than 10 employees are on different floors at any one time.

The Fire Precautions (Workplace) Regulations (1997)

These require every employer to carry out a risk assessment for the premises, under the **Management of Health and Safety Regulations (1999)**:

- Any obstacles that might hinder fire evacuation should be identified as problems areas.
- Suitable fire detection equipment should be in place, such as a **smoke alarm**.
- A method to warn of a fire should be in place, this might be an automatic alarm or trained employee shouting to raise the alarm.
- All escape routes should be clearly marked and free from obstacles.
- Fire-fighting equipment should be available and maintained, to be used only by those trained in its use.
- All employees should be trained in fire-evacuation practice and procedures.
- Fire-evacuation procedures should be reviewed regularly to account for changes to the staffing or premises. A fire drill should be carried out at least once a year to monitor evacuation procedures.

Never put yourself at risk – fires can spread quickly. Leave the building at once if in danger, and raise the alarm by telephoning the emergency services on the emergency telephone numbers, 999 or 112.

HEALTH AND SAFETY

Fire!
A fire can quickly get out of control. You do not have very long to act!
Fire drill notices should be visible to show people to the emergency exit route.
If there is a fire, never use a lift.

ACTIVITY

Fire exits
Fire exit doors must be clearly marked, be unlocked during working hours and be free from obstruction.

Fire-fighting equipment

Fire-fighting equipment must be available, located in a specified area. The equipment includes fire extinguishers, blankets, sand buckets and water hoses. Fire-fighting equipment should be used only when the cause of the fire has been identified – using the *wrong* fire extinguisher could make the fire worse. Different types of fire extinguishers are available to tackle different types of fire and colour coded according to type.

ACTIVITY

Fire extinguishers
Colour and symbols indicate the use of particular fire extinguishers. Make sure you know the meaning of each of the colours and symbols.

Cause of fire	Extinguisher type	Colour code
Electrical fire	Carbon dioxide (CO2)	Black
Solid material fire	Water	Red
Flammable liquids	Foam	Yellow
Electrical Fire	Dry-powder	Blue

There are four classes of fire: Class A, B, C and D. Symbols are used to identify these and choice of fire extinguisher

Fire extinguisher symbols Chubb Fire Ltd

Fire extinguishers Chubb Fire Ltd

Fire blankets Chubb Fire Ltd

Fire blankets are used to smother a small, localised fire or if a person's clothing is on fire. **Sand** is used to soak up liquids if these are the source of the fire, and to smother the fire. **Water hoses** are used to extinguish large fires caused by paper materials and the like – buckets of water can be used to extinguish a small fire. *Turn off the electricity first!*

It is important that you never use fire-fighting equipment unless you have been trained in its use.

ACTIVITY
Causes of fires Think of several potential causes of fire in the salon. How could each of these be prevented?

Other emergencies

Other possible emergencies that could occur relate to fumes and flooding. Learn the location of the water and gas stopcocks. In the event of a gas leak or a flood, the stopcocks should be switched off and the appropriate emergency service contacted.

Staff should also be trained in the procedures necessary for a bomb alert. This will involve recognising a suspect package, dealing with a bomb threat, evacuating staff and clients, and contacting the emergency services. Your local Crime Prevention Officer will advise on bomb security.

Insurance

Public liability insurance protects employers and employees against the consequences of death or injury to a third party while on the premises.

Product and **treatment liability insurance** is usually included with your public liability insurance but it is worth checking this with the insurance company.

All employers must have **employer's liability insurance**. This provides financial compensation to an employee who is injured as a result of a workplace accident. The Certificate of Insurance must be displayed indicating that a policy of insurance has been obtained.

PERSONAL HEALTH, HYGIENE AND APPEARANCE

HEALTH AND SAFETY

Drugs
If you take drugs, how might this affect your responsibilities under the implementation of the health and safety policy of your workplace?

Your appearance enables the client to make an initial judgement about both you and the salon, so make sure that you create the right impression! Employees in the workplace should always reflect the desired image of the profession they work in.

Professional appearance

Assistant therapist

Assistant therapists qualified to pre-foundation level will be required to wear a clean protective overall because they will be preparing the working area for client treatments and might also be involved in preparing clients.

Beauty therapist

The nature of many of the services offered requires beauty therapists to wear protective, hygienic clothing. A cotton overall is ideal; air can circulate, allowing perspiration to evaporate and discouraging body odour. Using a light colour such as white immediately shows the client that you are clean. A cotton overall might comprise a dress, a jumpsuit or a tunic top, with coordinating trousers.

Overalls should be laundered regularly and a fresh, clean overall worn each day.

Your appearance must create the right impression at all times   Dream Workwear

Receptionist

A receptionist employed solely to carry out reception duties might wear a different salon dress, complementary to those worn by the practising therapists. As the receptionist will not be as active, a smart jacket or cardigan might be appropriate. However, if the receptionist also carries out client services, the standard salon overall must be worn.

General rules for employees

Make-up

If you wear make-up, ensure it is attractive, and use the correct skin-care cosmetics to suit your skin type. A healthy complexion will be a positive advertisement for your work.

Jewellery

Keep jewellery to a minimum, such as a wedding ring, a watch and small earrings.

Nails

Nails should be short, neatly manicured and free of nail polish unless the employee's main duties involve nail treatments or reception duties. Artificial nails, if worn, must be short to avoid harm and ineffective treatment application during facial treatments.

Shoes

Wear flat, well-fitting, comfortable shoes that enclose the feet and complement the overall. Remember that you will be on your feet for most of the day!

Ethics

Beauty therapy has a **code of ethics**. Although not a legal requirement, this code can be used in criminal proceedings as evidence of improper practice. This is a code of behaviour and expected standards for the professional beauty therapist to follow.

Diet, exercise and sleep

A beauty therapist requires stamina and energy. To achieve this you need to eat a healthy, well-balanced diet, take regular exercise and have enough sleep.

ACTIVITY

Personal appearance
1 Collect pictures from various suppliers of overalls. Select those that you feel would be most practical for an assistant therapist (a Level 1 beauty therapist). Briefly describe why you feel these are the most suitable.
2 Design various hairstyles, or collect pictures from magazines, to show how the hair could be smartly worn by a therapist with medium-length to long hair.

ACTIVITY

Building stamina

1 Ask your tutor for guidelines before beginning this activity. Write down all the foods and drinks that you most enjoy. Are they healthy? If you are unsure, ask your tutor.
2 How much exercise do you take weekly?
3 How much sleep do you regularly have each night?
4 Do you think you could improve your health and fitness levels?

ACTIVITY

The importance of posture

1 Which treatments will be performed sitting, and which standing?
2 In what way do you feel your treatments would be affected if you were not sitting or standing correctly?

Posture

Posture is the way you hold yourself when standing, sitting and walking. *Correct* posture enables you to work longer without becoming tired, it prevents muscle fatigue and stiff joints, and it improves your appearance.

Good standing posture

If you are standing with good posture, this will describe you:

- head up, centrally balanced
- shoulders slightly back, and relaxed
- chest up and out
- abdomen flat
- hips level
- fingertips level
- bottom in
- knees level
- feet slightly apart and weight evenly distributed.

Good sitting posture

Sit on a suitable chair or stool with a good back support:

- sit with the lower back pressed against the chair back
- keep the chest up and the shoulders back
- distribute the body weight evenly along the thighs
- keep the feet together, and flat on the floor
- do not slouch, or sit on the edge of your seat.

Good posture – standing

Good posture – sitting

Step by step copyright 2006 Habia – all rights reserved.

Personal hygiene

It is vital that you have a high standard of personal **hygiene**. You are going to be working in close proximity with people. Bodily cleanliness is achieved through daily showering or bathing. This removes the stale sweat, dirt and bacteria that cause body odour. An antiperspirant or deodorant could be applied to the underarm area to reduce perspiration and thus the smell of sweat. Clean underwear should be worn each day.

Hands

Your hands and everything you touch are covered with germs. Although most are harmless, some can cause ill health or disease. Wash your hands regularly, especially after you have been to the toilet and before eating food. You must also wash your hands before and after treating each client, and during treatment if necessary. Washing the hands before treating a client minimises the risk of cross-infection and presents a hygienic, professional and caring image to the client.

Step by step: Handwashing

1 Wet your hands, wrists and forearms thoroughly using running water

2 Apply around 3ml to 5ml of liquid soap

3 Start the lathering process, rubbing palm to palm

4 Interlock fingers and rub, ensuring a good lather

5 Rub right hand over back of left, then left over right hand

6 Rub with fingers locked in palm of hand ensuring fingertips are cleaned

7 Lock thumbs and rotate hands

8 Grasp thumb with hand and rotate, repeat with opposite thumb

9 Rotate hand around wrist, repeat on opposite wrist

ACTIVITY

Hand hygiene
What further occasions can you think of when it will be necessary to wash your hands when treating a client?

HEALTH AND SAFETY

Soap and towels
Wash your hands with liquid soap from a sealed dispenser. Don't refill disposable soap dispensers when empty: if you do they will become a breeding ground for bacteria. Disposable paper towels or warm-air hand dryers should be used to dry the hands.

HEALTH AND SAFETY

Protecting yourself
You will be wise to have the relevant inoculations, including those against tetanus and hepatitis, to protect yourself against ill health and even death.

10 Rinse hands and wrists thoroughly using running water

11 Dry the hands and wrists thoroughly

12 Turn off the tap using a paper towel

13 Dispose of paper towel without touching any part of the waste bin

---

HEALTH AND SAFETY

Protecting the client
If you have any cuts or abrasions on your hands, cover them with a clean dressing to minimise the risk of secondary infection. Disposable gloves may be worn for additional protection.
Certain skin disorders are contagious. If the therapist is suffering from any such disorder they must not work, but must seek medical advice immediately.

TIP ✓

Fresh breath
When working, avoid eating strong-smelling highly spiced

HEALTH AND SAFETY +

Long hair
If long hair is not taken away from the face, the tendency will be to move the hair away from the face repeatedly with the hands, and this in turn will require that the hands be washed repeatedly.

ACTIVITY

Preventing the spread of infection
Think of different ways in which infection could be spread in the salon. In each case, what could be done to prevent the spread?

Feet

Keep your feet fresh and healthy by washing them daily and then drying them thoroughly. Deodorising foot powder may be used.

Teeth

Avoid bad breath by brushing your teeth at least twice a day and flossing them regularly. Use breath fresheners and mouthwashes as required to freshen your breath. Visit the dentist regularly, to maintain healthy teeth and gums.

Hair

Your hair should be clean and tidy. Have your hair cut regularly and shampoo and condition it as often as needed. If your hair is long, wear it off the face and taken to the crown of the head. Medium-length hair should be clipped back, away from the face, to prevent it falling forwards.

Hygiene in the workplace

Infections

Effective salon hygiene is necessary to prevent *cross-infection* and *secondary infection*. These can occur through poor practice, such as the use of implements that are not sterile. Infection can be recognised by the skin being red and inflamed, or pus being present.

Cross-infection occurs because some micro-organisms are contagious, that is, they can be transferred through personal contact – by touch or by contact with an infected instrument that has not been sterilised. **Secondary infection** can occur as a result of injury to the client during the treatment or, if the client already has an open cut, if bacteria penetrate the skin and cause infection. **Sterilisation** and **disinfection** procedures (see below) are used to minimise or destroy the harmful micro-organisms that could cause infection.

Infectious (contagious) diseases **contra-indicate** beauty treatment: they require medical attention. People with certain other skin disorders, even though these are not contagious, should likewise not be treated by the beauty therapist, as treatment might lead to secondary infection.

Sterilisation and disinfection

- **Sterilisation** is the total destruction of all living micro-organisms.
- **Disinfection** is the destruction of some, but not all, micro-organisms.

Sterilisation and disinfection techniques practised in the beauty salon involve the use of *physical* agents (e.g. radiation and heat) and *chemical* agents (e.g. antiseptics and disinfectants).

Radiation   A quartz mercury vapour lamp can be used as the source for **ultraviolet light**, which destroys micro-organisms. The object to be disinfected must be turned regularly so that the ultraviolet light reaches all surfaces. (Remember that ultraviolet light is of limited effectiveness and cannot be relied upon for sterilisation.)

The ultraviolet lamp must be contained within a closed cabinet. This cabinet is an ideal place for storing sterilised objects.

Heat   Dry and moist heat can both be used in sterilisation. One method is to use a dry **hot-air oven**. This is similar to a small oven, and heats to 150–180°C. It is seldom used in the salon.

More practical is a **glass-bead steriliser**. This is a small, electrically heated unit that contains glass beads: these transfer heat to objects placed in contact with them. This method of sterilisation is suitable for small tools such as tweezers and scissors.

An ultra-voilet light cabinet
Sorisa

HEALTH AND SAFETY

Sterilisation record
Ultraviolet light is dangerous, especially to the eyes. The lamp must be switched off before opening the cabinet. A record must be kept of usage, as the effectiveness of the lamp decreases with use.

An autoclave Depilex

Water is boiled in an **autoclave** (similar to a pressure cooker): because of the increased pressure, the water reaches a temperature of 121–134°C. Autoclaving is the most effective method for sterilising objects in the salon.

HEALTH AND SAFETY

Using an autoclave
Not all objects can safely be placed in the autoclave. Before using this method, check whether the items you wish to sterilise can withstand this heating process.
To avoid damaging the autoclave, always use distilled deionised water.
To avoid rusting, metal objects placed in the sterilising unit must be of good-quality stainless steel.

HEALTH AND SAFETY

Using disinfectant
Disinfectant solutions should be changed as necessary.
After removing the object from the disinfectant, rinse it in clean water to remove traces of the solution. (These might otherwise cause an allergic reaction on the client's skin.)

Disinfectants and antiseptics

If an object cannot be sterilised, it should be placed in a chemical **disinfectant** solution. A disinfectant destroys most micro-organisms, but not all. Hypochlorite is a disinfectant; bleach is an example of a hypochlorite. Hypochlorite is suitable for cleaning work surfaces but is unsuitable for metals as it is corrosive. Use as directed by the manufacturer's instructions.

An **antiseptic** prevents the multiplication of micro-organisms. It has a limited action and does not kill all micro-organisms. Because it is milder than a disinfectant, it can be used directly on the skin.

All sterilisation techniques must be carried out safely and effectively:

1 Select the appropriate method of sterilisation for the object. Always follow the manufacturer's guidelines on the use of the sterilising unit or agent.

2 Clean the object in clean water and detergent to remove dirt and grease. (Dirt left on the object might prevent effective sterilisation.)

3 Dry the object thoroughly with a clean, disposable paper towel.

4 Sterilise the object, allowing sufficient time for the process to be completed.

5 Place tools that have been sterilised in a clean, covered container.

Keep several sets of the tools you use regularly, so that you can carry out effective sterilisation.

Sterilisation tray with liquid
Ellisons

TIP

Surgical spirit
Before sterilisation, surgical spirit may be applied with clean cottonwool to clean small objects.

Workplace policies

Each workplace should have its own workplace policy identifying hygiene rules.

- Health and safety: follow the health and safety guidelines for the workplace.
- Personal hygiene: maintain a high standard of personal hygiene. Wash your hands with a detergent containing **chlorhexidine**.
- Cuts on the hands: always cover any cuts on your hands.
- Cross-infection: take great care to avoid cross-infection in the salon. Never treat a client who has a contagious skin disease or disorder, or any other contra-indication.

- Use hygienic tools: never use an implement unless it has been effectively sterilised or disinfected, as appropriate.
- Disposable products: wherever possible, use disposable products.
- Working surfaces: clean all working surfaces (such as trolleys and couches) with a chlorine preparation, diluted to the manufacturer's instructions. Cover all working surfaces with clean, disposable paper tissue.
- Gowns and towels: clean gowns and towels must be provided for each client. Towels should be laundered at a temperate of 60°C.
- Laundry: dirty laundry should be placed in a covered container.
- Waste: put waste in a suitable container lined with a disposable waste bag. A yellow '**sharps' container** should be available for waste contaminated with blood or tissue fluid.
- Eating and drinking: never eat or drink in the treatment area of the salon.
- Smoking: never smoke in the treatment area of the salon or other prohibited areas.
- Drugs and alcohol: never carry out treatments in the workplace under the influence of drugs or alcohol. Your competence will be affected putting yourself, clients and possibly colleagues at risk.

HEALTH AND SAFETY

Using chemical agents
Always protect your hands with gloves before immersing them in chemical cleaning agents, to minimise the risk of an allergic reaction.

SKIN DISEASES AND DISORDERS

The beauty therapist must be able to distinguish a healthy skin from one suffering from a skin disease or disorder. Certain skin disorders and diseases **contra-indicate** a beauty treatment: the treatment would expose the therapist and other clients to the risk of cross-infection. It is therefore vital that you are familiar with the skin diseases and disorders with which you might come into contact in the workplace. You will find further information relevant to the treatment area in Chapters 4 and 5.

Bacterial infections

Bacteria are minute single-celled organisms of varied shapes. Large numbers of bacteria inhabit the surface of the skin and are harmless (**non-pathogenic**); indeed some play an important positive role in the health of the skin. Others,

HEALTH AND SAFETY

Boils
Boils occurring on the upper lip or in the nose should be referred immediately to a physician. Boils can be dangerous when near to the eyes or brain.

TIP

HSE advice on cleaning
Advice on cleaning work surfaces and equipment can be found on COSHH Essentials webside: www.coshh-essentials.org.uk.

HEALTH AND SAFETY

Damaged equipment
Any equipment in poor repair must be repaired or disposed of. Such equipment may be dangerous and may harbour germs.

HEALTH AND SAFETY

Cuts on the hands
Open, uncovered cuts provide an easy entry for harmful bacteria, and may therefore lead to infection. Always cover cuts.

HEALTH AND SAFETY

Skin problems
If you are unable to identify a skin condition with confidence, so that you are uncertain whether or not you should treat the client, don't! Tactfully refer them to their physician before proceeding with the planned treatment.

Microscopic bacteria – streptococcus bacteria on the tongue, computer-coloured red/pink

David Gregory and Debbie Marshall/ Wellcome Photo Library

ACTIVITY

Search the internet for images of skin diseases and disorders. Start with www.dermatology.co.uk.

however, are harmful (**pathogenic**) and can cause skin diseases. Bacterial infections include:

- Impetigo: an inflammatory disease of the surface of the skin.
- Conjunctivitis or pink eye: inflammation of the mucous membrane that covers the eye and lines the eyelids.
- Hordeola or styes: infection of the sebaceous glands of eyelash hair follicles.
- Furuncles or boils: red, painful lumps, extending deeply into the skin.
- Carbuncles: infection of numerous hair follicles.
- Paronychia: infection of the tissue surrounding the nail.

Impetigo Dr M.H. Beck

Viral infections

Viruses are minute entities, too small to see even under an ordinary microscope. Viruses invade healthy body cells and multiply within the cell: in due course the cell walls break down, liberating new viral particles to attack further cells, and thus the infection spreads.

- Herpes simplex: a recurring skin condition, appearing at times when the skin's resistance is lowered through ill health or stress. It might also be caused by exposure of the skin to extremes of temperature or to ultraviolet light.
- Herpes zoster or shingles: in this painful disease, the virus attacks the sensory nerve endings. The virus is thought to lie dormant in the body and be triggered when the body's defences are at a low ebb.
- Verrucae or warts: small epidermal skin growths. Warts can be raised or flat, depending upon their position. There are several types of wart: plane, common and plantar.

Rob Young/Wellcome Photo Library

Microscopic virus – herpes simplex virus particles (orange) in the nucleus of an epithelial cell

Infestations

- Scabies or itch mites: a condition in which an animal parasite burrows beneath the skin and invades the hair follicles.
- Pediculosis capitis or head lice: a condition in which small parasites infest scalp hair.
- Pediculosis pubis: a condition in which small parasites infest body hair.
- Pediculosis corporis: a condition in which small parasites live and feed on body skin.

ACTIVITY

Avoiding cross-infection

List the different ways in which infection can be transferred in the salon.
How can you avoid cross-infection in the workplace?

Dr John Gray, *World of Skin Care*

Herpes simplex – a cold sore

Dr John Gray, *World of Skin Care*

Viral wart

Fungal diseases

Fungi are microscopic plants. They depend on their host for their existence. Fungal diseases of the skin feed off the waste products of the skin. Some fungi are found on the skin's surface; others attack the deeper tissues. Reproduction of fungi is by means of simple cell division or by the production of spores.

- Tinea pedis or athlete's foot: a common fungal foot infection.
- Tinea corporis or body ringworm: a fungal infection of the skin.
- Tinea unguium: ringworm infection of the fingernails.

Sebaceous gland disorders

The sebaceous glands are minute, sac-like organs in the skin. The cells of the glands produce the skin's natural oil – sebum.

- Milia: keratinisation of the skin over the hair follicle occurs, causing sebum to accumulate in the hair follicle. This condition usually accompanies dry skin.
- Comedones or blackheads: excess sebum and keratinised cells block the mouth of the hair follicle.
- Seborrhoea: excessive secretion of sebum from the sebaceous gland. This usually occurs during puberty, as a result of hormonal changes in the body.
- Steatomas, sebaceous cysts or wens: localised pockets or sacs of sebum that form in hair follicles or under the sebaceous glands in the skin. The sebum becomes stuck, the sebaceous gland becomes distended and a lump forms.
- Acne vulgaris: hormone imbalance in the body at puberty influences the activity of the sebaceous gland, causing an increased production of sebum. The sebum can be retained within the sebaceous ducts, causing congestion and bacterial infection of the surrounding tissues.
- Rosacea: excessive sebum secretion combined with a chronic inflammatory condition, caused by dilation of the blood capillaries.

Microscopic fungi – Penicilliam mould producing spores, plus very close up view of spore formation

David Gregory and Debbie Marshall, Wellcome Photo Library

Tinea pedis – athlete's foot

Dr A.L. Wright

Tinea corporis – body ringworm

Dr A.L. Wright

Comedones – blackheads

Dr A.L. Wright

Acne vulgaris

Dr John Gray, *World of Skin Care*

Rosacea

Dr John Gray, *World of Skin Care*

Dr John Gray, *World of Skin Care*

Derma Colour

Dr M.H. Beck

Dr M.H. Beck

Dr M.H. Beck

TIP ✓
Hyperpigmentation Hyperpigmentation may result from certain skin injuries,

Chloasmata caused by ultra-violet light damage over time

Vitiligo

TIP ✓
Vascular skin disorder If there is a vascular skin disorder, avoid overstimulating the skin or the problem will become more noticeable and the treatment may even cause further damage.

Pigmentation disorders

Pigmentation of the skin varies, according to the person's genetic characteristics. In general, the darker the skin, the more pigment is present, but some abnormal changes in skin pigmentation can occur:

- **Hyperpigmentation**: increased pigment production
- **Hypopigmentation**: loss of pigmentation in the skin.
- Ephelides or freckles: multiple, small pigmented areas of the skin. Exposure to ultraviolet light (as in sunlight) stimulates the production of melanin, intensifying their appearance.
- Lentigines: pigmented areas of skin, slightly larger than freckles, which do not darken on exposure to ultraviolet light.
- Chloasmata or liver spots: increased skin pigmentation in specific areas, stimulated by a skin irritant such as ultraviolet light. The condition often occurs during pregnancy and usually disappears soon after the birth of the baby. It might also occur as a result of taking the oral contraceptive pill. The female hormone oestrogen is thought to stimulate melanin production.
- Dermatosis papulosa nigra: often called flesh moles; characterised by multiple benign, small brown to black hyperpigmented papules, common in people with dark skins.
- Vitiligo or leucoderma: patches of completely white skin that have lost their pigment, or which were never pigmented.
- Albinism: the skin is unable to produce melanin and the skin, hair and eyes lack colour.
- Vascular naevi: there are two types of naevus of concern to beauty therapists: vascular and cellular. Vascular naevi are skin conditions in which small or large areas of skin pigmentation are caused by the permanent dilation of blood capillaries.
- Erythema: an area of skin in which blood capillaries have dilated, due either to injury or inflammation.
- Dilated capillaries: capillaries near the surface of the skin are permanently dilated.
- Spider naevi or stellate haemangiomas: dilated blood vessels, with smaller dilated capillaries radiating from them.
- Naevi vasculosis or strawberry marks: red or purplish raised marks that appear on the skin at birth.

Spider naevus – dilated blood vessels and capillaries

Strawberry naevus – port wine stain

Malignant melanoma – skin cancer

- Capillary naevi or port-wine stains: large areas of dilated capillaries that contrast noticeably with the surrounding areas.
- Cellular naevi or moles: skin conditions in which changes in the cells of the skin result in skin malformations.
- Malignant melanomas or malignant moles: rapidly growing skin cancers, usually occurring in adults.
- Junction naevi: localised collections of naevoid cells that arise from the mass production locally of pigment-forming cells (melanocytes).
- Dermal naevi: localised collections of naevoid cells.
- Hairy naevi: moles exhibiting coarse hairs from their surface.

HEALTH AND SAFETY +

Moles
If moles change in shape or size, if they bleed or form crusts, seek medical attention.

HEALTH AND SAFETY +

Skin tags
Skin tags often occur under the arms. In case they are present, take care when carrying out a wax depilation treatment in this area: do not apply wax over tags.

Skin disorders involving abnormal growth

- Psoriasis: patches of itchy, red, flaky skin, the cause of which is unknown.
- Seborrhoeic or senile warts: raised, pigmented, benign tumours occurring in middle age. These warts are not contagious, and are harmless.
- Verrucae filliformis or skin tags: these verrucae appear as threads projecting from the skin.
- Xanthomas: small, yellow growths on the surface of the skin.
- Keloids: these occur after skin injury. They are overgrown abnormal scar tissues, which spread and are characterised by excess deposits of collagen. To avoid skin discoloration the keloid must be protected from exposure to ultraviolet light.

Dr M.H. Beck

Psoriasis

Dr John Gray, *World of Skin Care*

Seborrhoeic or senile warts

Dr John Gray, *World of Skin Care*

Keloid scar on the neck

Dr A. L. Wright

Squamous cell carcinoma: aggressive, spreading cancer

Malignant (harmful) tumours

- Squamous cell carcinomas or prickle-cell cancers: malignant growths originating in the epidermis.
- Basal cell carcinomas or rodent ulcers: slow-growing malignant tumours that occur in middle age.

Dr A. L. Wright

Basal cell carcinoma: the commonest form of cancer, caused by ultraviolet light exposure

HEALTH AND SAFETY ➕

Record any known allergies
When completing the client record card, always ask whether your client has any known allergies.

Skin allergies

The skin can protect itself – to some degree – from damage or invasion. Any damage that occurs is detected by specialised **mast cells** that release the chemical **histamine** into the tissues. Histamine causes the blood capillaries to dilate, producing the reddening we call 'erythema'. The increased blood flow through these dilated capillaries brings materials in blood to the site of injury; these act to limit the damage and begin the process of repair.

If the skin is sensitive to and becomes inflamed on contact with a particular substance, this substance is called an **allergen**. Allergens can be animal, chemical or vegetable substances, and they can be inhaled, eaten or absorbed after contact with the skin. An **allergic skin reaction** appears as irritation, itching and discomfort, with reddening and swelling (as with nettle rash). If the allergen is removed, the allergic reaction subsides.

Everyone has different tolerances to the various substances we encounter in daily life. What causes an allergic reaction in one individual might be perfectly harmless to another. The following are just a few examples of allergens known to cause allergic skin reactions:

- metal objects containing nickel
- sticking plaster
- rubber
- lipstick containing eosin dye
- nail enamel containing formaldehyde resin

Dr M.H. Beck

Allergic reaction to a nickel button

Dr John Gray, *The World of Skin Care*

Allergic reaction to an ingredient in hair dye

Dr John Gray, *The World of Skin Care*

Allergic reaction to an antiperspirant

Dr John Gray, *The World of Skin Care*

Dr M.H. Beck

Dr M.H. Beck

Dermatitis caused by an irritant

Eczema

Uticaria – nettle rash

- hair and eyelash dyes
- lanolin, the skin moisturising agent
- detergents that dry the skin
- foods – well known examples are peanuts, cow's milk, lobster, shellfish and strawberries
- plants – such as tulips and chrysanthemums.

Common skin reactions include:

- Dermatitis: an inflammatory skin disorder in which the skin become red, itchy and swollen. There are two types of dermatitis. In *primary dermatitis* the skin is irritated by the action of a substance on the skin, and this leads to skin inflammation. In *allergic contact dermatitis*, the problem is caused by intolerance of the skin to a particular substance or groups of substances. On exposure to the substance the skin quickly becomes irritated and an allergic reaction occurs.
- Eczema: inflammation of the skin caused by contact, internally or externally, with an irritant.
- Urticaria (nettle rash) or hives: a minor skin disorder characterised by red, itchy patches caused by contact with an allergen, either internally (e.g. food or drugs) or externally (e.g. insect bites).

HEALTH AND SAFETY

Hypoallergenic products
The use of hypoallergenic products minimises the risk of skin contact with likely irritants.

HEALTH AND SAFETY

Allergies
You may suddenly become allergic to a substance that has previously been perfectly harmless. Equally, you may over time cease to be allergic to something.

HEALTH AND SAFETY

Infection following allergy
Following an allergic skin reaction in which the skin's surface has become itchy and broken, scratching may cause the skin to become infected with bacteria.

Glossary

Accident book	a written record of any accident in the workplace. Incidents in the accident book should be reviewed to see where improvements to safe working practice could be made
Antiseptic	a chemical agent that prevents the multiplication of micro-organisms. It has limited action and does not kill all micro-organisms
Autoclave	an effective method of sterilisation, suitable for small metal objects and beauty therapy tools. Water is boiled under increased pressure and reaches temperatures of 121–134°C
Bacteria	minute, single-celled organisms of various shapes. Large numbers live on the skin's surface and are not harmful (non-pathogenic); others, however, are harmful (pathogenic) and can cause disease
Contra-indication	a problematic symptom that indicates the treatment may not proceed
Control of Substances Hazardous to Health (COSHH) (2002)	these regulations require employers to identify hazardous substances used in the workplace and state how they should be correctly store and handled
Controlled Waste Regulations 1992	categorises waste types. The Local Authority provides advice on how to dispose of waste types in compliance with the law.
Cosmetic Products (Safety) Regulations (2004)	part of consumer protection legislation that requires that cosmetics and toiletries are safe in their formulation and are safe for use for their intended purpose as a cosmetic and comply with labelling requirements
Cross-infection	the transfer of contagious micro-organisms
Disinfectant	a chemical agent that destroys most micro-organisms
Electricity at Work Regulations (1989)	these regulations state that electrical equipment in the workplace should be tested every 12 months, by a qualified electrician. The employer must keep records of the equipment tested and the date it was checked
Erythema	reddening of the skin
Fire Precautions (Workplace) Regulations (1997)	this legislation requires that every employer must carry out a risk assessment for the premises in relation to fire evacuation practice and procedures under the Management of Health and Safety Regulations (1999)
Fire Precautions Act (1971)	legislation that states that all staff must be familiar with and trained in fire and emergency evacuation procedures for their workplace
Fungi	microscopic plants. Fungal diseases of the skin feed off the waste products of the skin. They are found on the skin's surface or they can attack deeper tissues
Hazard	a hazard is something with potential to cause harm
Health and Safety (Display Screen Equipment) 1992	these regulations cover the use of visual display units (VDUs) and computer screens. They specify acceptable levels of radiation emissions from the screen and identify correct posture, seating position, permitted working heights and rest periods.
Health and Safety (First Aid) Regulations (1981)	legislation that states that workplaces must have appropriate and adequate first-aid provision
Health and Safety at Work Act (1974)	legislation that lays down the minimum standards of health safety and welfare requirements in all workplaces
Health and Safety policy	each employer of more than five employees must have a written health and safety policy issued to their employees outlining their health and safety responsibilities

Glossary

Histamine	a chemical released when the skin comes into contact with a substance that it is allergic to. Cells called mast cells burst, releasing histamine into the tissues. This causes the blood capillaries to dilate, which increases blood flow to limit skin damage and begin repair
Hygiene	the recommended standard of cleanliness necessary in the salon to prevent cross-infection
Hyperpigmentation	increased pigment production
Hypopigmentation	loss of pigmentation
Infestation	a condition where animal parasites live off and invade a host
Legislation	laws affecting the beauty therapy business relating to products and services, the business premises and environmental conditions, working practices and those employed
Management of Health and Safety at Work Regulations (1999)	this legislation provides the employer with an approved code of practice for maintaining a safe, secure working environment
Manual Handling Operations (1992)	legislation that requires the employer to carryout a risk assessment of all activities undertaken which involve manual handling (lifting and moving objects)
Personal Protective Equipment (PPE) at Work Regulations (1992)	this legislation requires employers to identify through risk assessment those activities that require special protective equipment to be worn.
Posture	the position of the body, which varies from person to person. Good posture is when the body is in alignment. Correct posture enables you to work longer without becoming tired; it prevents muscle fatigue and stiff joints.
Provision and Use of Work Equipment Regulations (PUWER) (1998)	this regulation lays down important health and safety controls on the provision and use of equipment
Reporting of Injuries, Diseases and Dangerous Occurrences Regulations (RIDDOR) (1995)	these regulations require the employer to notify the local enforcement officer in writing, in cases where employees or trainees suffer personal injury at work.
Risk	a risk is the likelihood of a hazard's potential being realised
Secondary infection	bacterial penetration into the skin causing infection
Skin allergy	if the skin is sensitive to a particular substance an allergic skin reaction will occur. This is recognised by irritation, swelling and inflammation.
Sterilisation	the destruction of all micro-organisms
Ultraviolet light (UVL) cabinet	a unit that uses ultraviolet light to sanitise small objects. Objects must be clean before placing in the cabinet, and must be turned so that the ultraviolet light rays effectively strike each surface of the object.
Viruses	the smallest living bodies – too small to see under an ordinary microscope. Viruses invade healthy body cells and multiply within the cell. Eventually the cell walls break down and the virus particles are freed to attack further cells.
Workplace (Health Safety and Welfare) Regulations (1992)	these regulations provide the employer with an approved code of practice for maintaining a safe, secure working environment

Assessment of knowledge and understanding

Unit G1: Ensure your own actions reduce risks to health and safety (mandatory unit)

You have now learnt about the health and safety responsibilities for everyone in the workplace. This will enable you to ensure your own actions reduce risks to health and safety. To test your level of knowledge and understanding, answer the following short questions. These will prepare you for your summative (final) assessment.

Action to avoid health and safety risks

1 What are your main legal responsibilities under the Health and Safety at Work Act (1974)?

2 Give five examples of good personal presentation in maintaining health and safety in the salon?

3 Why is your personal conduct important to maintain the health and safety of yourself and colleagues and clients?

4 Why must you always be aware of and look for hazards in the workplace?

5 What do you understand by these terms?
   a sterilisation
   b disinfection

6 Name a piece of equipment that is used in the work place for sterilisation and disinfection.

7 What do you understand by good posture, and why is it important for you to consider when working?

8 You have been asked to check the contents of the first aid box, what should it contain?

Dealing with significant risks in your workplace

1 In your workplace, think of the main risks that could occur and what precautions you could take to safe guard yourself and others?

2 While cleaning a wax heater you notice that the wires in the lead are exposed. What action should you take?

3 If you were unable to deal with a risk (because it was outside your area of responsibility) what action would you take?

4 What does the abbreviation COSHH stand for? Why is it important to follow the supplier's and manufacturer's instructions for the safe use of materials and products?

5 When cleaning the area after wax depilation treatment, what personal protective equipment should you wear and how should waste be disposed of?

6 You notice that a large box containing stock has been left in front of a fire exit, why is it important that this is removed?

7 It is a heavy box but you will be able lift it. What is the correct lifting technique to lift an object from the ground?

Taking the right action in the event of a danger

1 What is the procedure for dealing with an accident in the workplace?

2 What is a fire drill? What is the fire evacuation procedure in your workplace? How often should this be carried out?

3 In the event of a real fire, after having safely evacuated the building, how would you contact the appropriate emergency service?

4 In reception, you discover a smoking bin in which a fire has started because of an un-extinguished cigarette. How should this fire be extinguished?

5 What action should be taken in the event of a gas leak?

chapter 2

G2 Assist with salon reception duties

Learning objectives

This chapter covers the skills and knowledge you need to help with salon reception duties. These include maintaining the reception area in a clean and tidy manner, looking after clients on arrival and departure, dealing with enquiries and scheduling appointments. It describes the competencies to enable you to:

- maintain the reception area
- attend to clients and enquiries
- help to make appointments for salon services.

At all times whilst assisting with reception duties it is important to consider all health and safety requirements using the knowledge you have gained from unit G1: Ensure your own actions reduce risks to health and safety (see Chapter 1).

Elemis Day Spa reception Elemis

PRACTICAL SKILLS AND KNOWLEDGE

This table will help you to check your progress in gaining the necessary practical skills and knowledge for Unit G2: Assist with salon reception duties.

Tick (✓), when you feel you have gained your practical skills and knowledge in the following areas:

Practical skills and knowledge checklist	✓
1 Maintaining the reception area	
2 Maintaining reception product displays including the removal of any faulty products	
3 Knowing when and whom to report low levels of reception stationery and retail stock	
4 Salon policy for reception client hospitality	
5 Using good verbal and non-verbal communication and listening skills to suit the situation	
6 Dealing with enquiries efficiently and competently	
7 Knowing when to refer enquiries on and to whom	
8 How to accurately record messages taken and when to pass on information and to whom	
9 Legal storage and access of client records in relation to the Data Protection Act (1998)	
10 How to efficiently deal with requests for appointments face to face or by telephone	
11 Ensuring all appointment details are recorded legibly, correctly and confirmed for accuracy with the client as per salon policy	
12 Knowing when to refer appointment requests on and to whom	
13 To have a good understanding of salon services, products and pricings	

When you have ticked all the areas you can, ask your assessor to assess you on Unit G2: Assist with salon reception duties. After practical assessment, your assessor might decide that you need to practise further to improve your skills. If so, your assessor will tell you how and where you need to improve to gain competence.

When working on reception, make sure clients get the right impression

THE RECEPTION AREA

The salon **reception** gives clients their first (and also their final) impression of the salon, whether this is on the telephone or in person on a visit to the salon. First impressions count, so make sure that clients get the *right* impression!

Outcome 1: Maintain the reception area

UNIT G2

Maintain the reception area

1. Ensure that the reception area is clean and tidy at all times

2. Ensure that product displays are clean, well stocked and appealing to the eye at all times

3. Report shortages of reception resources, e.g. stationery, price lists or retail products, to the supervisor

4. Remove any faulty or damaged products and equipment from the reception area following health and safety best practice. Report immediately to the supervisor

5. Show good client care and hospitality

It is your responsibility to keep the reception area tidy and organised, and to be organised and pleasant when assisting with reception duties. The different duties you will be expected to perform are listed below.

A receptionist

Assist with salon reception duties

Keep the reception area clean and tidy
Display areas should be clean and well stocked

↓

Report shortages of reception resources and retail products

↓

Identify and inform supervisor of faulty or damaged
equipment and products

↓

Show good client care and hospitality at all times

↓

Refer any enquiries you are unable to deal with
to the relevant person

↓

Accurately take messages and pass these on promptly

↓

Comply with the Data Protection Act (1998)
regarding client records

↓

Handle appointments immediately,
accurately identify client requirements

↓

Record all details accurately in the correct place and confirm
appointment details with the client

↓

Refer any appointments you are unable to deal
with to the relevant person

TIP ✔

Client attention
It is important to pay clients the right amount of attention – according to their specific requirements – to ensure client satisfaction. This must always be considered in a busy situation when clients might be kept waiting. Communicate with clients regularly to keep them updated if they are waiting for a service.

Reception equipment and resources

The reception area should be uncluttered. The main equipment and furnishings required for an efficient reception include:

- A reception desk: the size of the desk will depend on the size of the salon; some salons have several receptionists. The desk should include shelves and drawers, and some have an in-built lockable cash or security drawer. The desk should be at a convenient height for the client to write a cheque. It should also be large enough to house the appointment book or computer (or both).

- A comfortable chair: the receptionist's chair should provide adequate back support.

- A computer: these are becoming more and more popular in salons because they can perform so many functions. They can be used to store data about clients, to keep appointment schedules, to carry out automatic stock control, and to record business details such as accounts and marketing information. Some computers can even be programmed to recommend specific treatments on the basis of personal data about the client.

- A calculator: this is used for simple financial calculations, especially if the salon does not have a computer.

- Stationery: this should include price lists, gift vouchers, appointment cards and a receipt pad.

Saks, Covent Garden

HEALTH AND SAFETY

Eating and drinking
The receptionist and other employees should not eat or drink at reception, nor should they smoke.

TIP

Price lists
Some salons put their price list in booklet form, detailing the treatments offered and explaining their benefits.

TIP

File contact details
Visitors to the salon might leave a business card, stating the name of their company, and the representative's name, address and telephone number. The receptionist should file these cards for future reference. Contact details are often stored electronically if the salon has a computer.

TIP

Protect the floor
Have an attractive, heavy-duty mat at the entrance to reception to protect the main floor-covering. Vacuum the mat when necessary during the day to keep the reception looking attractive.

- A notepad: for taking notes and recording messages.
- An address and telephone book: this should hold all frequently used telephone numbers.
- A telephone and answering machine: this allows clients to contact you, even when the salon is closed, with appointment requests or even to let you know about an unavoidable change or cancellation: you can then re-schedule appointments as quickly as possible.
- Record cards: these confidential cards record the personal details of each client registered at the salon. They should be kept in alphabetical order in a filing cabinet or a card-index box, and should be ready for collection by the therapist when treating new or existing clients. Each card records:
  - ◆ the client's name, address and telephone number
  - ◆ any medical details
  - ◆ any contraindications (such as allergies and contra-actions)
  - ◆ treatment aims and outcomes
  - ◆ services received, products used, and retail products purchased.
- Pens, pencils and an eraser: make sure these stay at the desk!
- A display cabinet: this can be used to store products, and any other merchandise sold by the salon; these items are referred to as retail products.

ACTIVITY

Planning a reception area
Design a reception area (to scale) appropriate to a small or large beauty salon. Discuss the choice of wall and floor coverings, furnishings and equipment, and give the reasons for their selection. Consider client comfort, and health and safety.

Retail products

Retail sales are very important to the beauty salon. They are a simple way of greatly increasing the income without too much extra time and effort. Clients need to be informed about the retail products available. The retail display area should be kept well stocked and clear.

Maintain the appearance of the display area and retail stock by regularly:

A nail product display   Jessica Nail

- Dusting the display shelving and stock. If the salon is located on a busy main road it will quickly become dusty. Take care not to damage the packaging during cleaning.
- Rearrange the displays regularly to maintain client interest, for the promotion of new products and if products have been popular and the display needs to be restocked.
- Rotate the stock so that if new items arrive they will go to the back of the display shelf, and older ones are used first.
- Write down any damages to retail products. Damage can be recognised by spoilt packaging caused by leakage or damage to the container of the product. Inform your supervisor.

- Report any shortages of retail stock or reception resources and pass onto your supervisor. Keep accurate and up-to-date records.
- If there are testers for the client to try, ensure these are kept clean and in good condition.

Check that all the reception equipment and resources are available, including retail products. Any shortages must be reported to the supervisor immediately. This ensures the smooth running of the reception area.

Client hospitality

Hospitality is friendliness and how you welcome your client to the salon.

Hospitality is important and shows the salon's commitment to client care. If a client arrives early for an appointment, or is likely to be delayed, offer a magazine or a refreshment such as coffee or water; magazines should be renewed regularly. It is also a pleasant gesture to have boiled sweets on reception for clients.

TIP

Video facilities
Video facilities in reception can be used to promote salon services. If your salon provides this facility, make sure video material is played regularly.

CLIENT RECORDS

Client record cards record personal details of each client registered at the salon. They should be kept in alphabetical order, if not stored electronically on a computer, and should be ready for collection by the beauty therapist on the client's arrival for an appointment.

The Data Protection Act (1998)

This legislation is designed to protect the client's privacy and confidentiality. It is necessary to ask the client questions before the treatment can be finalised and the information obtained is recorded on the client record card. All information about a client is confidential and should be stored in a secure area following client treatment. This is usually at reception. When assisting with reception duties, you must only pass the client's confidential information to authorised people, and you must always store client records securely.

HEALTH AND SAFETY

Cleaning
A large salon might employ a cleaner to maintain the hygiene of the reception area. In a smaller salon this might be the responsibility of the receptionist or a beauty therapist. Reception must be maintained to a high standard at all times.

THE RECEPTIONIST

Outcome 2: Attend to clients and enquiries

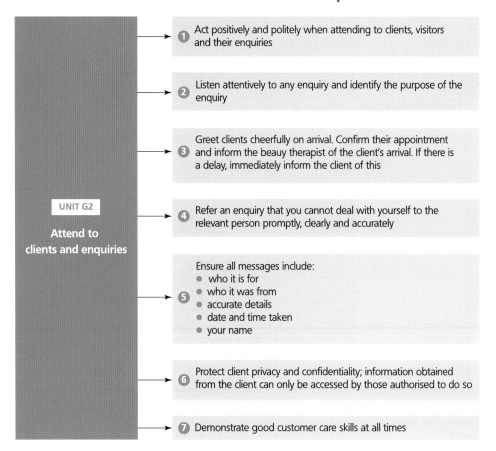

UNIT G2

Attend to clients and enquiries

1. Act positively and politely when attending to clients, visitors and their enquiries

2. Listen attentively to any enquiry and identify the purpose of the enquiry

3. Greet clients cheerfully on arrival. Confirm their appointment and inform the beauy therapist of the client's arrival. If there is a delay, immediately inform the client of this

4. Refer an enquiry that you cannot deal with yourself to the relevant person promptly, clearly and accurately

5. Ensure all messages include:
   - who it is for
   - who it was from
   - accurate details
   - date and time taken
   - your name

6. Protect client privacy and confidentiality; information obtained from the client can only be accessed by those authorised to do so

7. Demonstrate good customer care skills at all times

Receptionists should have a smart appearance and be able to communicate effectively and professionally, thereby creating the right impression.

As an assistant receptionist, your duties include:

- maintaining the reception area
- looking after clients on arrival and departure
- assisting with scheduling appointments
- dealing with enquiries
- telling the appropriate beauty therapist that a client or visitor has arrived
- assisting with retail sales within your level of responsibility.

TIP ✓

Wear a badge
It is a good idea for receptionists to wear a badge indicating their name and position.

TIP ✓

Be polite
If you are engaged on the telephone when a client arrives, look up and acknowledge the client's presence.

TIP ✓

Be careful not to interrupt when passing on information
If you need to pass information to another beauty therapist, never interrupt a client service. Wait until a suitable point in the treatment to communicate. If urgent information needs to be passed on, do so with minimum disruption. Make a note of what the message is and from whom to avoid forgetting!

The assistant receptionist should know:

- the name of each member of staff, their role and their area of responsibility
- the salon's hours of opening, and the days and times when each therapist is available
- the range of services or products offered by the salon, and their cost
- who to refer to if you receive different enquiries that you are unable to deal with or are not within your area of responsibility
- the person in your salon to whom you should refer reception problems
- any current discounts and special offers that the salon is promoting
- the benefits of each treatment and each retail product
- the approximate time taken to complete each treatment
- how to schedule follow-up treatments.

You will also need to consider the last three points when completing Unit BT1: Prepare and maintain the beauty therapy work area.

HEALTH AND SAFETY

Keep the reception clear
As the receptionist, you should be familiar with the emergency procedure in case of fire. Make sure the reception area is free from any obstacles that could block the exit route in the event of an emergency. This will also remove potential hazards that may cause an accident

Communication with clients

All clients should feel valued. A client can be made to feel uncomfortable, ignored or special – and this can happen without you saying anything! Even without speaking you communicate by body language: with your eyes, your face and your body passing on some of your feelings. This is called **non-verbal communication**. How you look and how you behave in front of your clients is important. On meeting a client, always smile, make eye contact and greet them cheerfully – however bad your day is!

Verbal communication occurs when you talk directly to another person, either face to face or over the telephone. Always speak clearly and precisely, and avoid slang. It is important to be a good listener: this will help you identify what the client wants and understand their personality.

Avoid all controversial topics such as sex, religion and politics. Never gossip with clients.

The following verbal and non-verbal **communication skills** are desirable in a receptionist:

- the ability to behave positively and confidently
- speak clearly
- have a friendly and smiling approach
- paying enough attention to the client and maintaining eye contact
- good listening skills
- demonstrating interest in everything that is going on around the reception area
- giving each client individual attention and respect.

ACTIVITY

Reception experiences
Pair with a colleague and share your experiences of a well managed and a badly managed reception.

ACTIVITY

Non-verbal communication
In conversation, you give signals that tell others whether you are listening or not.
What do you think the following signals indicate?
- a smile
- head tilted, and resting on one hand
- eyes looking around you
- eyes semi-closed
- head nodding
- fidgeting.
Can you think of other body signals that indicate whether you are interested or not?

Dealing with a dissatisfied client at reception

Occasionally, a client might be dissatisfied. The receptionist is usually the first contact with the client and you might have to deal with dissatisfied, angry or

TIP

If you behave calmly, the client will become less angry. If you become angry, the client will become even angrier

ACTIVITY

Do's and don'ts
List five important do's and five don'ts for the receptionist.

ACTIVITY

Reception scenarios
With colleagues, consider the following situations that might occur when working as a receptionist. What would you do in each situation?
- A client arrives very late for an appointment but insists that she is treated.
- A client questions the bill.
- A client comes in to complain about a treatment given previously.

awkward customers in a public place. Considerable skill is needed if you are to deal constructively with a potentially damaging situation.

Never become angry or awkward yourself. Always remain courteous and tactful, and communicate confidently and politely.

- Listen to the client as they describe their problems, without making judgement. Do not make excuses for yourself or for colleagues.
- Ask questions to check that you have the full background details.
- If possible, agree on a course of action, offering a solution if you can. Check that the client has agreed to the proposed course of action. It might be necessary to consult the salon manager before proposing a solution to the client: if you're not sure, always check first.
- Log the complaint following salon policy recording: the date, the time, the client's name, the nature of the complaint and the agreed course of action.

MAKING APPOINTMENTS

Making correct entries in the appointment book or salon computer is one of the most important duties of the receptionist. As assistant receptionist, you must familiarise yourself with the salon's appointment system, column headings, treatment times and any abbreviations used for the treatments.

Each beauty therapist will have their name at the head of a column. Entries in columns must not be reallocated without the consent of the therapist, unless they are absent, when a senior therapist would reallocate the client bookings to ensure minimum disruption.

Outcome 3: Help to make appointments for salon services

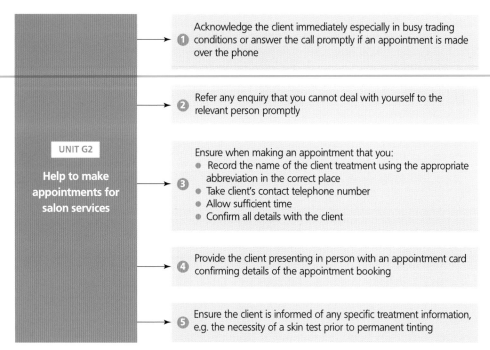

UNIT G2

Help to make appointments for salon services

1. Acknowledge the client immediately especially in busy trading conditions or answer the call promptly if an appointment is made over the phone

2. Refer any enquiry that you cannot deal with yourself to the relevant person promptly

3. Ensure when making an appointment that you:
   - Record the name of the client treatment using the appropriate abbreviation in the correct place
   - Take client's contact telephone number
   - Allow sufficient time
   - Confirm all details with the client

4. Provide the client presenting in person with an appointment card confirming details of the appointment booking

5. Ensure the client is informed of any specific treatment information, e.g. the necessity of a skin test prior to permanent tinting

Information required

When clients call to make an appointment, their name and the desired treatment service should be recorded. Allow adequate time to carry out the required service. Take the client's telephone number in case the therapist falls ill or is unable to keep the appointment for some other reason. If the client requests a particular therapist, be sure to enter the client's name in the correct column.

The hours of the day are recorded along the left-hand side of the appointment page, divided into 15-minute intervals. You need to know how long each treatment takes so that you can allow sufficient time for the therapist to carry out the treatment in a safe, competent, professional manner. If you don't allow sufficient time, the therapist will run late and this will affect all later appointments. On the other hand, if you allow too much time, the therapist's time will be wasted and the salon's earnings will be less than they could be. Suggested times to be allowed for each service are given in the treatment chapters. See the table on the next page for a breakdown of treatments and their abbreviations and times allowed.

Confirm the name of the therapist who will be carrying out the treatment, the date and the time.

Finally, confirm or estimate the cost of the treatment to the client.

You could offer an **appointment card** to the client, to confirm the appointment. The card should record the treatment, the date, the day and the time. The therapist's name might also be recorded.

Treatments are usually recorded in an abbreviated form. Everyone who uses the appointment page must be familiar with these abbreviations.

> **HEALTH AND SAFETY**
>
> **Health and Safety (Display Screen Equipment) Regulations (1992)**
> These regulations cover the use of visual display units (VDUs) and computer screens. They specify acceptable levels of radiation emissions from the screen and identify correct posture, seating position, permitted working heights and rest periods.

Treatment service timings

Treatment	Abbreviation	Treatment time allowed
Cleanse and make-up	C/M/up	45 minutes
Eyebrow shaping	E/B reshape or trim	15 minutes
Eyebrow tint	EBT	10 minutes
Eyelash tint	ELT	20 minutes
Eyelash perm	ELP	45 minutes
Manicure	Man	45 minutes
Nail art	N/Art	5–10 minutes (per nail)
Pedicure	Ped	45 minutes
Waxing eg:	half	$\frac{1}{2}$ leg wax 30 minutes
	three-quarter	$\frac{3}{4}$ leg wax 30–40 minutes
	full	Full leg wax 50 minutes
Bikini wax	B/wax	15 minutes
Underarm wax	U/arm wax	15 minutes
Forearm wax	F/arm wax	30 minutes
Eyebrow wax	E/B wax	15 minutes
Ear pierce	E/P	15 minutes
Facial	F	60 minutes
False lashes	F/Lash	20 minutes

Treatment abbreviations and times allowed for various treatments

If an appointment book is used, write each entry neatly and accurately. It is preferable to write in pencil: appointments can be amended by erasing and rewriting, keeping the book clean and clear.

Appointments can be made up to six weeks in advance. Often, clients will book their next appointment as they leave the current appointment. How far ahead the receptionist is able to book appointments will vary from salon to salon.

When clients arrive for their treatment, draw a line (or tick) through their name to indicate that they have arrived.

DAY SATURDAY		DATE 17th MARCH	
THERAPIST	JANE	SUE	LIZ
9.00	Mrs Young		
9.15	½ Leg wax	Jenny Heron	
9.30	Carol Green	ELT DEBT	
9.45	Full Leg wax	Hair trim	
10.00	B / wax		
10.15		Sandra Smith	Fiona Smith
10.30	Mrs Lord E/B wax	C / M / UP	C / M / UP
10.45			strip lash
11.00		Mrs James	
11.15		u/arm wax	
11.30		f/arm wax	Carol Brown
11.45			DNA
12.00			
12.15			
12.30	Jeanette Raffell		
12.45	man .		
1.00	ped.		
1.15		Sue Yip E/P	
1.30	½ Leg wax	T. Scott	
1.45		¾ Leg wax	
2.00	Liz Whiteside	u/arm wax	
2.15	facial		
2.30			
2.45			Pat King
3.00			C / M / UP
3.15	Ann Wood		man.
3.30	man ,		
3.45	E/B Reshape		
4.00			

A page from the appointment book

If a client cancels, indicate this on the appointment page *immediately*, usually with a large C written through the booking. This enables another client to take the appointment.

If a client fails to arrive, the abbreviation DNA (did not arrive) is usually written over the booking. The client should then be telephoned to see if a rebooking is required.

Some salons have a policy of charging for a missed appointment.

SKIN SENSITIVITY (PATCH) TESTS

A skin sensitivity (patch) test

Before clients receive certain treatments it might be necessary to carry out skin tests. The skin test is often carried out at reception, and the receptionist or assistant therapist will be able to perform the test, after training. Every client should undergo a skin test before a permanent tinting treatment to the eyelashes or eyebrows, or perming of the eye lashes. Further tests might be necessary, depending on the client's sensitivity, before treatments such as artificial eyelash treatment or wax depilation.

TELEPHONE CALLS: COMMUNICATION

First impressions count. Good telephone technique can win clients; poor technique can lose them. Here are some guidelines for good technique:

- Answer quickly: on average, callers are willing to wait up to nine seconds: try to respond to the call within six seconds.
- Be prepared: have information and writing materials ready to hand. It should not normally be necessary to leave the caller waiting while you find something.
- Be welcoming and attentive: speak clearly, without mumbling, at the right speed. Pronounce your words clearly, and vary your tone. Sound interested, and never abrupt.

Remember: the caller may be a new client ringing round several salons. The decision whether to visit *your* salon might depend on your attitude and the way you respond to the call.

> **TIP** ✓
>
> **Your telephone manner**
> Don't regard the phone ringing as an interruption. Always remember that clients matter – they ensure the success of your business!
> A client who has received a poor response to a telephone call might tell friends or colleagues about it. If you receive an enquiry and are not sure of the answer, ask for help from a person with the relevant experience. Tell the client politely that you are unable to help but will get somebody who can.

> **ACTIVITY** 🏃
>
> **Telephone calls**
> A telephone call is often the first contact the client has with the salon and is an important method of communication.
> - How should the phone be answered?
> - What should you confirm if the client requires an eyelash tint?
> - What action would you take if there was not sufficient time for the appointment at the time requested?

Use good telephone technique

TIP

Cordless/mobile phones
If the salon uses a cordless or a mobile phone, keep this in a central location where it can easily be found when it rings. After each call, be sure to return the phone to its normal location.

ACTIVITY

Communicating with clients
Listen to experienced receptionists and notice how they communicate with clients.

ACTIVITY

Listening to yourself
A pleasant speaking voice is an asset. Do you think you could improve your speech or manner?
Record your voice as you answer a telephone enquiry, then play it back. How did you sound? This is how others hear you!

TIP

Personal calls
Check the salon's policy on personal calls. Usually they are permitted only in emergencies. This is so staff are not distracted from clients and to keep the telephone free for clients to make appointments.

Here are some more ideas about good telephone technique:

- Smile – this will help you put across a warm, friendly response to the caller.
- Speak clearly and alter the pitch of your voice as you speak, to create interest.
- As you answer, give the standard greeting for the salon, for example 'Good morning, Bodyworks Beauty Salon, Susan speaking. How can I help you?'
- Listen attentively to the caller's questions or requests. You will be speaking to a variety of clients: you must respond appropriately and helpfully to each.
- Consider the information the caller gives you and be sure to respond to what has been said or asked.
- Use the client's name, if you know it; this personalises the call.
- Summarise the main requests from the call to yourself; ask for further information if you need it.
- At the end, repeat the main points of the conversation clearly to check that you and the client have understood each other.
- Close the call pleasantly, for example 'Thank you for calling, Mrs Smith. Goodbye.'

If you receive a business call, or a call from a person seeking employment, always take the caller's name and telephone number. Your supervisor can then deal with the call as soon as they are free to do so.

Transferring calls

If you transfer a telephone call to another extension, explain what you are doing and thank the caller for waiting. If the extension to which you have transferred the call is not answered within nine rings, tell the caller that you will ask the person concerned to ring back as soon as possible. Take the caller's name and telephone number.

Taking messages

It is important that messages are recorded correctly and are passed on at the right time.

Messages should be recorded on a memorandum ('memo') pad. Each message should record:

- who the message is for
- who the message was from
- the date and the time the message was received
- accurate details of the message
- the telephone number or address of the caller
- the signature of the person who took the message.

When taking a message, repeat the details you have recorded so that the caller can check that you've got it right. Pass the message to the correct person as soon as possible.

```
┌─────────────────────────────────────────────────────┐
│            TELEPHONE MESSAGE RECEIVED                 │
│                                                       │
│  To: Angela              Date: 10.07.07               │
│                                                       │
│  From: Jenny Heron       Time: 9:30 am                │
│                                                       │
│  Number: 273 451         Taken by: Sandra             │
├─────────────────────────────────────────────────────┤
│                    Positional                         │
│                                                       │
│  Please could you ring Jenny Heron                    │
│  regarding her appointment on                         │
│  Saturday.                                            │
│                                                       │
│                                                       │
└─────────────────────────────────────────────────────┘
```

A memo

ACTIVITY

Finding the right approach
What telephone manner should you adopt when dealing with people who are:
- angry?
- talkative?
- nervous?
- confused?

THE PAYMENT POINT

Every beauty therapy or cosmetic business will have a policy for handling cash and for operating the payment point. It is important that you are given training and are confident to take payment in the client's preferred method, which might be cash or cash equivalent, e.g. gift voucher, cheque or payment card. You will be required to handle cash if you study salon reception duties at Level 2.

Glossary

Appointment	arrangement made for a client to receive a service on a particular date and time
Communication	exchange of information and the development of understanding between people
Computer	electronic machine that holds data on the business
Data Protection Act (1998)	legislation designed to protect client privacy and confidentiality
Health and Safety (Display Screen Equipment) Regulations (1992)	these regulations cover the use of visual display units and computer screens. They specify acceptable levels of radiation emissions from the screen and correct working posture, permitted working heights and rest periods
Hospitality	friendliness and care for clients at reception
Messages	communication of information to another person in written or verbal form
Non-verbal communication	communicating using body language, i.e. using your eyes, face and body transmitting your feelings
Reception	an area in the salon where clients are received and their enquiries dealt with, either in person or by telephone
Record card	personal information recorded for each client, recording treatments received and retail product purchases
Resources	needs of various kinds, people, stock, facilities
Retail	selling of goods, i.e. products that clients use at home
Skin sensitivity (patch) test	assessment of a client's tolerance/sensitivity to a particular substance
Verbal communication	occurs when you talk directly to another person, either face to face or over the telephone

Unit G2: Assist with salon reception duties

You have learnt how to maintain the reception area, attend to clients and their enquiries, and make appointments for salon services. The skills developed enable you to professionally assist with salon reception duties. To test your level of knowledge and understanding, answer the following questions. These will prepare you for your summative (final) assessment.

Maintain the reception area

1 You have a responsibility to handle client records when assisting with reception. What legislation must you comply with when handling this confidential information?

2 State three duties of the salon receptionist.

3 What is your role in maintaining the reception area?

4 Name five pieces of equipment or resources required for the reception area, and state the purpose of each.

5 If, as assistant receptionist, you were unable to give appropriate information to a client, what action would you take?

6 How can you make a client feel welcomed at reception? Give three examples of good client hospitality.

7 When making an appointment for a client, what information should be obtained from the client?

Attend to clients and enquiries

1 When taking a message, what five things should be recorded?

2 What do you understand by the following methods of communication:
- verbal communication
- non-verbal communication

3 Give three examples of positive body language.

4 If a client was dissatisfied with a treatment they had received, how would you deal with this client?

5 Give three examples of good telephone technique.

6 If a client is likely to be delayed for an appointment, who will you need to communicate with and with what regularity?

Help to make appointments for salon services

1 Why is it important that you know the salon services available and their treatment cost and duration?

2 How can you assist in increasing the sales of retail products?

3 What action would you take if you found stock to be spoilt when restocking the display area?

4 Why is it important to notify your supervisor if you notice low stock levels of reception resources, i.e. price lists?

5 When making an appointment for a client requesting a specific day/time:

- what do you need to check initially in the appointment book?
- what information do you need to obtain from the client?

chapter 3

BT1 Prepare and maintain the beauty therapy work area

Learning objectives

This chapter covers the skills and knowledge you need to prepare and maintain the beauty therapy work area for waxing, eye treatments, make-up, manicure, pedicure and facial treatments. It will help you to learn the materials and equipment that are required for each treatment service. The chapter also describes the competencies you will need to:

- **prepare the beauty therapy work area**
- **maintain the beauty therapy work area.**

When preparing and maintaining the beauty therapy work area, it is important to consider all health and safety requirements using the knowledge you have gained from Unit **G1: Ensure your own actions reduce risks to health and safety** (see Chapter 1).

EzFlow

Everything you do reflects on the salon

PRACTICAL SKILLS AND KNOWLEDGE

This table will help you to check your progress in gaining the necessary practical skills and knowledge for Unit BT1: Prepare and maintain the beauty therapy work area. Tick (✓), when you feel you have gained your practical skills and knowledge in the following areas:

Practical skills and knowledge checklist　　　　　　　　　　　　　　　✓

1 The environmental conditions for **each** treatment, including:
- lighting
- heating
- ventilation
- general comfort

2 Selecting and using the correct method of disinfection/sterilisation for tools and equipment required

3 Preparing the treatment area for **waxing** following all health and safety requirements

4 Preparing the treatment area for **eye treatments** following all health and safety requirements

5 Preparing the treatment area for **make-up** following all health and safety requirements

6 Preparing the treatment area for **manicure** following all health and safety requirements

7 Preparing the treatment area for **pedicure** following all health and safety requirements

8 Preparing the treatment area for **facial treatment** following all health and safety requirements

9 Personal presentation and hygiene is maintained at all times

10 Positive communication skills are used when liaising with clients and colleagues

11 Obtaining client's records efficiently

12 Correct methods of waste removal and disposal are followed

13 Manufacturers' guidelines for the care and maintenance of equipment are followed

14 Efficient cleaning and tidying of the work area ready for further treatments

15 Correct storage of client records following treatment in compliance with the Data Protection Act 1998.

When you have ticked all the areas you can, ask your assessor to assess you on Unit BT1: Prepare and maintain the beauty therapy work area. After practical assessment, your assessor might decide that you need more practice to improve your skills. If so, your assessor will tell you how and where you need to improve to gain competence.

PREPARING AND MAINTAINING THE BEAUTY THERAPY AREA

As a Level 1 beauty therapist it is a requirement that you support your colleagues by providing assistance with services delivered to clients. One of your roles is to prepare and maintain the working areas for the following beauty therapy treatments:

- waxing
- eye treatments
- make-up
- manicure
- pedicure
- facial.

Preparing and maintaining the beauty therapy area includes:

Sterilisation/disinfection of the equipment before treatment

↓

Ensuring the environmental conditions are correct for treatment

↓

Disinfecting work surfaces to be used

↓

Preparation of work area
Ensuring all equipment and materials are available

↓

Providing the client record card for the therapist

↓

Disposal of waste immediately following treatment

↓

Secure storage of the client record card

↓

Tidying the work area and preparing it for further treatment

ACTIVITY

Treatment timings

Sometimes more than one area of waxing is required. How long would you allow for a client receiving:

- half-leg, bikini and underarm wax
- full-leg, bikini and underarm wax
- eyebrow and facial wax.

RECEPTION

You need to allow sufficient time to prepare the work area for each treatment. Check the appointment book schedule regularly to see what treatment is next.

Allow at least 10 minutes to make sure you have all the equipment, materials and products necessary for the treatment. Certain pieces of equipment might have preparation requirements. For example, wax must be heated before use. Allow sufficient time for this, so that the equipment is available for use.

It is important to know how long each treatment service takes so that you are available to tidy the treatment area when it has finished.

Treatment service timings

Treatment service	Length of treatment
Waxing:	
eyebrow wax	15 minutes
underarm wax	15 minutes
half leg wax minutes	30 minutes
bikini line wax	15 minutes
arm wax	30 minutes
full leg	50 minutes
Eye treatments:	
eyebrow shape	15 minutes
eyelash tint	20 minutes
eyebrow tint	10 minutes
eyelash perming	45 minutes
false lashes	20 minutes
Make-up	45 minutes
Manicure	45 minutes
Pedicure	45 minutes
Facial	60 minutes

TIP ✔

Client record card

- You are responsible for collecting the client record card before treatment and for storing it again after treatment.
- The client's personal details are confidential. It is important that you comply with the **Data Protection Act (1998)**: all information relating to a client should be stored securely and only those staff with permission should be able to access it. So, as soon as all treatment details have been recorded on the record card it should be put back into secure storage.
- Do not leave client record cards lying about!

Ellisons

In addition to the treatment service timings listed above you are required to assist with facial and nail treatments as part of your Level 1 qualification, allow the following times for these treatments:

facial treatment   45 minutes

nail treatment   45 minutes

A description of each treatment service follows, with explanations of how to prepare and maintain each treatment working area. For each service it is important that hygienic practice is considered before preparing the beauty therapy work area and during its maintenance. This will help prevent cross-infection – the transfer of harmful bacteria/micro-organisms from one person to another.

Depending on the equipment required for each beauty therapy service, they can be prepared hygienically either by disinfection or by sterilisation methods:

- **Sterilisation** destroys all living micro-organisms
- **Disinfection** destroys some, but not all, micro-organisms.

An autoclave is used when small pieces of equipment need to be sterilised. This heats water to a temperature of 121–134°C. Metal objects and some sponge materials can be sterilised in an autoclave.

Disinfection is achieved by placing small pieces of equipment – often plastic, which is unsuitable for the high temperatures achieved in the autoclave – in a chemical disinfectant or in an ultraviolet cabinet.

Hygiene checks

- Ensure that all tools and equipment are clean and sterile before use.
- Disinfect work surfaces regularly.
- Use disposable items whenever possible. Discard immediately after use in a covered, lined waste container.
- Follow hygienic practices.
- Maintain a high standard of personal hygiene.

An autoclave   Depilex

An ultraviolet light cabinet
Ellisons

PREPARE AND MAINTAIN THE BEAUTY THERAPY WORK AREA

Chemical disinfectant   Ellisons

Outcome 1: Prepare the beauty therapy work area

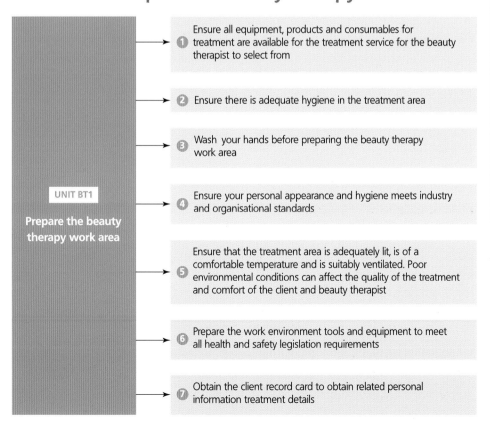

UNIT BT1

Prepare the beauty therapy work area

1 Ensure all equipment, products and consumables for treatment are available for the treatment service for the beauty therapist to select from

2 Ensure there is adequate hygiene in the treatment area

3 Wash your hands before preparing the beauty therapy work area

4 Ensure your personal appearance and hygiene meets industry and organisational standards

5 Ensure that the treatment area is adequately lit, is of a comfortable temperature and is suitably ventilated. Poor environmental conditions can affect the quality of the treatment and comfort of the client and beauty therapist

6 Prepare the work environment tools and equipment to meet all health and safety legislation requirements

7 Obtain the client record card to obtain related personal information treatment details

Outcome 2: Maintain the beauty therapy work area

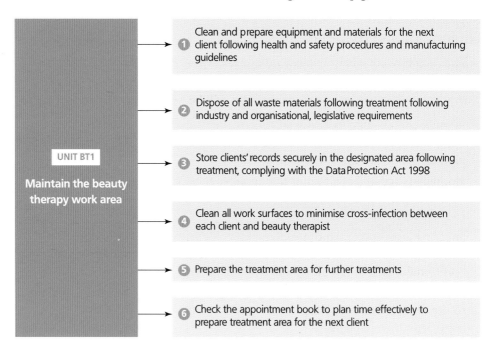

UNIT BT1

Maintain the beauty therapy work area

1. Clean and prepare equipment and materials for the next client following health and safety procedures and manufacturing guidelines

2. Dispose of all waste materials following treatment following industry and organisational, legislative requirements

3. Store clients' records securely in the designated area following treatment, complying with the Data Protection Act 1998

4. Clean all work surfaces to minimise cross-infection between each client and beauty therapist

5. Prepare the treatment area for further treatments

6. Check the appointment book to plan time effectively to prepare treatment area for the next client

PREPARING AND MAINTAINING THE BEAUTY THERAPY WORK AREA FOR WAXING

Wax treatment involves using wax to remove hairs temporarily from the face and body. Waxing removes both the visible hair and the root, so the re-growth is completely new, soft, fine hairs. It will be 4–6 weeks before the client requires the service again.

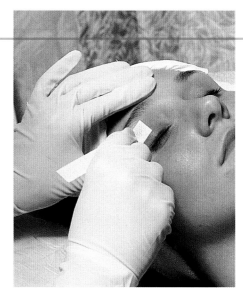

Waxing the eyebrows

Pretreatment

Equipment and materials

There are different wax formulations and systems available for use. Your salon might use only one, or more than one system. Select and prepare the choice of wax as guided by the beauty therapist who will be performing the treatment:

- Warm wax is heated in a special, low-temperature heater to around 43°C, when it becomes runny. Warm waxes are frequently made of mixtures of glucose syrup or honey, and zinc oxide.

- Hot wax is applied at a higher temperature than warm wax – around 50°C. Blocks or pellets of solid wax are heated in a special heater until a thickish, runny consistency is achieved.

- Sugaring is an ancient and popular method of hair removal. A mixture of sugar, lemon and water is applied as a paste, called **sugar paste**, or as a traditional warm wax called **strip sugar**.

- The roller system uses warm wax contained in cartridges, which are heated to the correct working temperature. A disposable applicator head is provided for each client.

Refer to the equipment and materials checklist on p. 57 to make sure you have everything that is needed for the waxing treatment.

Honey wax   Ellisons

Sterilisation and disinfection

- Small metal tools should be sterilised after use. Clean them with surgical spirit and clean cotton wool and then sterilise them in the autoclave. They should be stored in the ultraviolet cabinet after sterilisation to keep them sterile and ready for use.

- Towels should be boil washed at 60° to destroy harmful micro-organisms and prevent cross-infection.

- Wash your hands before handling clean equipment.

Hot wax discs   Salon System

Sugar paste   Ellisons

Strip sugar, disposable spatulas and muslin strips   Moom

Sugar wax designed for men's hair removal Moom

Waxing system with disposable roller heads Clean + Easy

HEALTH AND SAFETY

Personal Protective Equipment (PPE) at Work Regulations (1992)
There is a risk of contact with body fluids during waxing. It is recommended that special protective equipment is worn when handling contaminated equipment and waste. This includes surgical gloves made of nitrile or PVC formulations.
It is the employer's responsibility to make these available to employees; it is the employee's responsibility to wear them.

HEALTH AND SAFETY

Prevent cross-infection
If you have a cut on your hand you should wear a protective sterile dressing to prevent cross-infection.

EQUIPMENT AND MATERIALS CHECKLIST FOR WAXING

	Warm wax	Hot wax	Roller wax	Strip sugar	Sugar paste
Couch – with sit-up and lie-down positions and an easy-to-clean surface	☐	☐	☐	☐	☐
Trolley – to hold all the necessary equipment and materials	☐	☐	☐	☐	☐
Protective plastic couch cover	☐	☐	☐	☐	☐
Disposable tissue roll to cover the trolley surface and couch	☐	☐	☐	☐	☐
Disposable wooden spatulas – a selection of different sizes used for application of wax to different body parts	☐	☐		☐	
Wax removal strips (bonded fibre) cut to size for the waxing service	☐	☐		☐	
Talcum powder (purified) to prevent the wax from sticking to the skin, to make fair hair more visible		☐			☐
Cotton wool pads, to cleanse and apply products to the skin	☐	☐	☐	☐	☐
Facial tissues, to protect client's clothing and to blot the skin dry after cleansing and after wax application	☐	☐	☐	☐	☐
Skin cleanser (pre-wax lotion) to remove surface dirt, cosmetic products, dead skin and body oils	☐	☐	☐	☐	☐
Surgical spirit or a commercial cleaner designed to clean equipment	☐	☐	☐	☐	☐
Towels for protecting the client's clothing and for modesty when clothing has been removed	☐	☐	☐	☐	☐
Small scissors for trimming long hairs before waxing	☐	☐	☐	☐	☐
A jar of disinfecting solution to hold small metal tools, e.g. scissors	☐	☐	☐	☐	☐
Tweezers for removing stray hairs	☐	☐	☐	☐	☐
Petroleum jelly to cover areas that must not be waxed, e.g. moles	☐	☐	☐	☐	☐
Wax	Select according to organisations' therapist's preferred system				
Wax heater, set at recommended temperature (as appropriate)					
Afterwax lotion with soothing, healing and cooling properties, to be applied after hair removal	☐	☐	☐	☐	☐
Mirror (clean) – for facial waxing	☐	☐	☐	☐	☐
Apron – to protect workwear from wax spillages	☐	☐	☐	☐	☐
Disposable surgical gloves – used when waxing the underarm and bikini areas.	☐	☐	☐	☐	☐
Bin (swing top) – lined with a disposable polythene bin liner	☐	☐	☐	☐	☐
Client record card – to record client's personal details before and after treatment	☐	☐	☐	☐	☐
Aftercare leaflets – to provide guidance notes for the client to follow after treatment	☐	☐	☐	☐	☐

HEALTH AND SAFETY

Storing liquids

To prevent damage to the electrical equipment and electric shock to the beauty therapist, liquids must not be stored next to electrical equipment. Keep any liquids on another shelf on the trolley.

Waxing trolley Beauty Express

TIP

Jobs for the day

One of your first tasks at the start of the day will be to switch on the wax heater so that it is ready for the first client. Forgetting to do this will cause unnecessary delay.

How to prepare the work area

1 The area should be clean and tidy.

2 Check the temperature of the working area: the client must not be too warm or they will perspire, which will affect adherence of the wax to the skin. Increase ventilation in the treatment area as necessary.

3 There should be a clean, empty covered bin in the treatment area, lined with a polythene bin liner.

4 Disinfect all work surfaces and cover them with clean, disposable paper tissue.

5 Check the trolley to make sure it contains everything that is needed to carry out the treatment.

6 Collect metal tools, e.g. scissors and tweezers from the ultraviolet cabinet and put them into a disinfecting solution on the trolley.

7 The wax must be at a suitable temperature for use: heated as recommended by the manufacturer according to wax type, allow sufficient time for this.

- **warm wax** is heated in a heater or cartridge to between 43°C and 48°C – when it should be warm and fluid in consistency
- **hot wax** is heated to 50°C
- **strip sugar** wax is heated to 43–48°C
- **sugar paste** is heated in the microwave or heater, following the manufacturer's guidelines, until it is soft
- an individual cartridge of **roller wax** is heated on a medium setting in a heating and storage compartment until it reaches a fluid consistency.

8 The couch should be covered with a clean plastic protective sheet. Disposable paper-tissue bedroll should be placed over the plastic sheet for additional protection and comfort.

9 Place a towel neatly on the couch to protect the client's clothing and to cover them when they have undressed.

10 Position the couch according to the treatment part to be treated. The couch should be in the sit-up position, unless the client is only having their bikini line or underarm areas waxed, in which case it should be flat.

11 Collect the client's record card and place on the treatment trolley.

12 Confirm that preparation of the work area meets with the Senior Therapist's satisfaction.

Post treatment

Clean, tidy and prepare the work area in a suitable condition for further treatments.

- Dispose of used wax materials after use.
- If the roller wax system has been used, replace the disposable applicator with a new one, ready for the next client.

- Clean the wax heaters using equipment cleaner, if there are any wax spillages.
- Dispose of the paper-tissue bedroll.
- Wipe the plastic couch cover with surgical spirit and clean cotton wool to remove any wax spillages.
- Empty the bin that was used to collect waste in the treatment area. Replace the polythene bin liner with a new one.
- Remove used metal tools from the treatment area so that can be sterilised.
- Disinfect work surfaces.
- Disposable waste from waxing might have body fluids on it; potentially it is a health risk. It must be handled, collected and disposed of according to the COSHH procedures, training by the employer and local environment agency in accordance with the Controlled Waste Regulations 1992. It is a good idea to wear disposable protective gloves when cleaning up and disposing of waste products and materials after treatment; they will help protect you from contact with body fluids.

> **HEALTH AND SAFETY**
>
> **Contaminated waste**
> A yellow sharps container or heavy duty yellow sac should be available for waste contaminated with blood or tissue fluids.

Other post treatment actions

- Check the wax level in the different wax heaters regularly, and replenish with new wax as necessary. This should be done in advance of the next treatment application so that the wax is at the correct temperature and working consistency and sufficient to carry out at the next service.
- Protective towels should be removed from the treatment area and should be laundered.
- Return the client record card to the secure storage area for client data.
- At the end of the working day, switch off the wax heater if this system has been used.

PREPARING AND MAINTAINING THE BEAUTY THERAPY WORK AREA FOR EYE TREATMENTS

Eye treatment involves preparation for any of the following treatments:

- eyebrow shaping
- eyelash and eyebrow permanent tinting
- false lash application, either strip lashes or individual lashes
- eyelash perming.

Eyebrow shaping

Eyebrow shaping treatment involves removing the brow hair, to maintain a shape or create a new shape. Hairs are removed using small metal tools called tweezers. There are two types – manual and automatic:

- manual tweezers remove stray hairs and are used to accentuate the brow shape

Automatic tweezers Ellisons

Manual tweezers Ellisons

TIP ✓
Brow hairs Brow hairs can be removed quickly using wax, which is basically mass tweezing.

- automatic tweezers (as shown in the photos of tweezing below) are designed to remove the bulk of excess hair, they have a spring-loaded action.

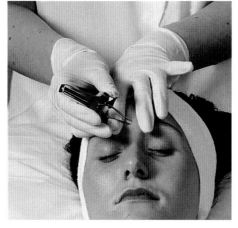

Tweezing at the bridge of the nose with automatic tweezers

Tweezing at the outer corner of the eyebrow

Eyelash and eyebrow tinting

The hairs of the eyelashes and brows are permanently coloured using a dye to enhance the appearance of the eye area. The tinting treatment can be performed on the eyelashes, the eyebrow area or to both.

Processing the eyelash tint

Removing eyebrow tint from the eyebrow

False lashes

False lashes are threads of artificial hair attached to the client's natural lashes, imitating the natural eyelashes and making them appear longer and thicker. There are two types – semi-permanent individual lashes and strip lashes:

- strip lashes, are designed to be worn for a short time period, e.g. a day
- individual lashes can be worn for 4–6 weeks.

Positioning the strip lash to the base of the natural lashline

Applying an individual lash to the upper lid

Eyelash perming

Eyelash perming treatment uses a perming lotion formulated for use around the eyes to permanently curls the lashes, making them appear longer. The effect lasts as long as the growth cycle of the hair. Hairs grow, die are shed and are replaced by a new hair.

Applying the perm lotion to the eyelashes

Covering the lashes with lint-free pads as the product works to permanently curl the hair

Sterilisation and disinfection

- Small metal tools should be sterilised after use. Clean them with surgical spirit and clean cotton wool and then sterilise them in the autoclave. Store them in the ultraviolet cabinet after sterilisation, ready for use.
- Applicators for permanent tinting and eyelash perming should be disposable, and thrown away after use.
- Towels and headbands should be boil washed to destroy harmful micro-organisms and prevent cross-infection.
- Wash your hands before handling clean equipment.

> **TIP** ✓
>
> **Sterilised tweezers**
> Always have more than one pair of sterilised tweezers available. A clean, sterile pair will be required if the beauty therapist drops the tweezers they are using on the floor.

Pretreatment

Refer to the equipment and materials checklist to make sure that you have all that is required to perform eye treatment.

EQUIPMENT AND MATERIALS CHECKLIST FOR EYE TREATMENTS

	Eyebrow Shaping	Permanent Tinting	False Lash Application	Eyelash Perming
Couch – with sit-up and lie-down positions and an easy-to-clean surface	☐	☐	☐	☐
Trolley – to hold all the necessary equipment and materials	☐	☐	☐	☐
Medium-sized towels to protect the client's clothing	☐	☐	☐	☐
Disposable tissue roll to cover the trolley surface	☐	☐	☐	☐
Headband to protect the client's hair from any chemical treatments and to keep hair away from the treatment area	☐	☐	☐	☐
Non-oily eye make-up remover to cleanse the eye area (to prevent it causing a barrier to the treatment)	☐	☐	☐	☐
Damp cotton wool for cleansing the treatment area, removing treatment products and to protect the skin	☐	☐	☐	☐
Facial tissues, for blotting dry the skin/lashes	☐	☐	☐	☐
Magnifier lamp (cold) to enlarge the appearance of the treatment area when performing eyebrow shaping	☐			
Disposable wooden spatulas to remove cosmetic products from containers		☐		
Cotton buds to apply and remove products from the area	☐	☐	☐	☐
Tweezers – manual or automatic	☐		☐	
Disposable surgical gloves; these should be worn when performing an eyebrow shape to avoid contact with body tissue fluids. They also protect the hands against contact with chemicals that could cause skin irritation	☐			☐
A jar of disinfecting solution to hold small metal tools	☐	☐		
Antiseptic cleansing lotion to prepare and sanitise the area before brow hair removal	☐			
Soothing antiseptic lotion or cream to reduce redness and assist skin healing following brow hair removal	☐			

	Eyebrow shaping	Permanent tinting	False lash application	Eyelash perming
Coloured permanent tints, available in black, brown, blue and grey		☐		
Hydrogen peroxide – 10 vol, 3% strength		☐		
Petroleum jelly, to protect the skin from staining during eyelash tinting		☐		
Eye shields to protect from staining or chemical irritation		☐		☐
Non-metallic bowl to mix the permanent tint and hydrogen peroxide		☐		
Disposable brushes to apply the permanent tint		☐		
Surgical spirit to wipe the points of the tweezers to remove artificial eyelash adhesive			☐	
Eyelash adhesive for strip lashes. Eyelash adhesive for individual lashes			☐	
Strip eyelash lengths in a selection of colours and lengths Individual lashes in a selection of colours and lengths			☐	
Eyelash adhesive solvent for the removal of individual false lashes			☐	
Scissors to trim the length of the strip lash			☐	
Sterilised small dish lined with foil to place the eyelash adhesive in during lash application			☐	
Mild eyelash perm solution to curl the hair				☐
Fixing lotion to make the new eyelash curl permanent				☐
Eyelash curler – a selection of different sizes to curl the natural lashes around during the curling process				☐
Eyelash adhesive to secure short lashes to the eyelash curler				☐
Lint-free pad to remove the perm and fixing lotion				☐
Disposable cocktail sticks to fix the hairs into the correct position around the eyelash curler				☐
Disposable brushes or cotton buds to apply the perm lotion and fixing lotion				☐
Hand mirror (clean) to discuss and agree the treatment plan and show the client the results	☐	☐	☐	☐
Bin (swing-top) lined with a disposable bin liner	☐	☐	☐	☐
Client's record card so that the client's details can be recorded before and after treatment	☐	☐	☐	☐

Beauty Express

Ellisons

Ellisons

Ellisons

Ellisons

Ellisons

Sonisa

Ellisons

HEALTH AND SAFETY ✚

Storing chemicals safely
Do not put chemicals such as eyelash perm lotion near a wax heater on the trolley. The heat could affect the quality (and performance) of the chemicals and they could even become dangerous if they are flammable.

Make sure you follow the COSHH (Control of Substances Hazardous to Health) guidelines on how equipment should be stored (see Chapter 1).

Preparing the work area

1 The area should be clean and tidy.

2 Check the temperature of the working area: the client must not be too warm. Increase ventilation as necessary.

3 There should be a clean, empty covered bin in the treatment area lined with a polythene bin liner.

4 Disinfect all work surfaces and cover with clean, disposable, paper tissue.

5 Check the trolley to make sure it contains everything that will be needed to carry out the treatment.

Eyelash perming products Ellisons

Eyelash tinting products Ellisons

False lashes Ellisons

Eyebrow shaping tweezers Ellisons

6 Collect metal tools from the ultraviolet cabinet, put them into a disinfectant solution on the trolley.

7 Prepare cotton wool: provide a selection of damp and dry cotton wool on the trolley, usually in small bowls.

8 Display the materials and products required for the eye treatment.

9 The beauty couch or chair should be protected with a long strip of disposable bedroll or a freshly laundered sheet and bath towel.

10 For eye treatments the treatment couch should be slightly elevated, not flat.

11 A small towel should be placed neatly at the head of the couch – this will be draped across the client's chest for hygiene and protection during the treatment. The bedroll or sheet will need to be changed, and freshly laundered towels replaced, before the next client.

12 Collect the client's record card and put it on the treatment trolley.

13 Confirm that preparation of the work area meets with the Senior Therapist's satisfaction.

Post treatment

Clean, tidy and prepare the work area in a suitable condition for further treatments.

- Dispose of the paper-tissue bedroll.
- Empty the bin that was used to collect waste in the treatment area. Replace the bin liner with a new one.
- Clean small bowls used to hold cotton wool in hot, soapy water; rinse the bowls and dry.
- It is a good idea to wear disposable protective gloves when cleaning up and disposing of waste products and materials after treatment. Gloves help to avoid skin staining from permanent tint treatment and skin irritation from contact with chemicals used in the treatment.
- Clean small metal tools with surgical spirit and clean cotton wool before sterilising them in the autoclave.
- Protective towels should be removed from the treatment area and laundered.
- Disinfect work surfaces..
- Return materials to the store area; ideally chemicals should be stored in a cool, dark, locked cupboard. Check that all bottle lids are securely closed to prevent spillage and loss of product quality.

  If a product requires to be disposed of i.e. the eyelash tint tube is empty, inform the relevant person for stock control before disposal and replacement. This will ensure adequate stock levels are maintained.
- Return the client record card to the secure storage area for client data.

TIP ✔

Cleaning bowls
Care should be taken when cleaning bowls used for permanent tint, as the tint product will stain any materials it comes into contact with. Do not use your salon treatment towels as they could be permanently stained.

TIP ✔

False lashes
False lashes may be required if applying an evening make-up or if extra definition is required for the eye area. Ask the beauty therapist if she will be requiring these. Place on the trolley if required.

PREPARING AND MAINTAINING THE BEAUTY THERAPY WORK AREA FOR MAKE-UP TREATMENT

 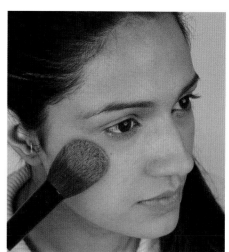

Make-up treatments

Make-up is used to enhance the skin and facial features to help us appear and feel more attractive. Skilful application of different cosmetic products can reduce or emphasise facial features and so create balance in the face. The overall effect should suit the client and reflect her personality, lifestyle and the occasion for which the make-up is to be worn.

A large number of make-up products are available and a range should be available for the beauty therapist to select from to achieve the required effect.

Sterilisation and disinfection

- Ensure tools and equipment are clean and sterile before use.
- Where possible, disposable applicators are used during make-up application, costing these into the treatment price. Make-up brushes if used should be cleaned after each use and stored in the ultraviolet cabinet, ready for use.
- There should be at least three sets of make-up brushes available to allow for disinfection after each use.
- Make-up sponges should be cleaned and disinfected after use, dried and stored in the ultraviolet cabinet, ready for use.
- The make-up palette should be placed in the ultraviolet cabinet after cleaning, ready for use.
- Cosmetic pencils should be sharpened before each use to expose a fresh clean surface.
- Towels should be boil washed to destroy harmful micro-organisms and prevent cross-infection.
- Wash your hands before handling clean equipment.

Pretreatment

Refer to the equipment and materials checklist to make sure that you have all that is required for make-up treatment.

EQUIPMENT AND MATERIALS CHECKLIST FOR MAKE-UP TREATMENT

Sonisa — Couch or beauty chair with sit-up and lie-down positions and an easy-to-clean surface ☐

Sonisa — Trolley to hold all the necessary equipment and materials ☐

Sonisa — A medium-sized towel to protect the client's clothing ☐

Ellisons — Disposable tissue roll to cover the trolley surface ☐

Ellisons — Head-band to protect the client's hair and to keep hair away from the treatment area ☐

Ellisons — Hair clips to keep the client's hair away from the treatment area. These can be used in preference to a head-band.
Note: If the client has had her hair styled before make-up application, hair clips (in preference to a head-band) will avoid spoiling the hair whilst offering protection from make-up products ☐

Ellisons — Eye make-up remover – non-oily to cleanse the eye area to ensure effective make-up application and that the make-up will last ☐

Salon Systems — Cleansing lotion – a range available to suit the different skin types
Normal, dry, combination, oily, sensitive ☐

Toning lotion – a range available to suit the different skin types
Normal, dry, combination, oily, sensitive ☐

Silhouette-Dermalift — Moisturiser – a range available to suit the different skin types ☐
Normal, dry, combination, oily, sensitive ☐
Note: Moisturiser should be a light formulation to give the make-up durability

Sonisa — Magnifying lamp to inspect the skin more closely following cleansing ☐

EQUIPMENT AND MATERIALS CHECKLIST FOR MAKE-UP TREATMENT

Ellisons

Damp and dry cotton wool prepared for each client to apply and remove cleansing and make-up products ☐

Ellisons

Large white facial tissues to blot the skin after facial toning, and to protect the skin during make-up application ☐

Bowls to hold the prepared cotton wool ☐

Bin (swing-top) lined with a disposable bin liner ☐

Ellisons

Make-up a range, suitable for clients with known allergies to cosmetics, contact lens wearers, for different skin types and colours, including: concealing and contouring cosmetics ☐

- foundations
- eye shadows
- mascara
- lipsticks
- translucent powders
- eyeliners
- brow liners
- lip glosses
- lip liners

Ellisons

Make-up brushes (assorted) to apply make-up products ☐

Ellisons

Disposable applicators and brushes, for example for the application of lipstick, eye shadow and mascara ☐

Moom

Cosmetic sponges for foundation application ☐

Make-up palette for preparing cosmetics prior to application ☐

Ellisons

Pencil sharpener for cosmetic pencils ☐

Spatulas to remove products from containers ☐

Ellisons

Orange sticks to remove products from containers ☐

Mirror (clean) to show the client the effects achieved ☐

Ellisons

Client record card to record client's details before and after treatment ☐

HEALTH AND SAFETY

Disinfection in the ultraviolet cabinet
Allow 20 minutes exposure for each side of an object disinfected in the ultraviolet cabinet. Thus 40 minutes is required for effective disinfection.

Preparing the work area

1 The area should be clean and tidy.

2 There should be a clean covered, empty bin in the treatment area lined with a polythene bin liner.

3 Disinfect all work surfaces and cover with clean, disposable, paper tissue.

4 Check the trolley to make sure it has all that is needed to carry out the treatment.

Range of make-up products   Ellisons

5 Collect make-up tools from the ultraviolet cabinet, brushes, palette and sponges and place on the trolley.

6 Prepare cotton wool: provide a selection of damp and dry cotton wool placed on the trolley, usually held in small bowls.

7 Adjust the lighting – the room should be well lit for make-up application.

8 Check the room temperature. Good ventilation is important – it should not be too warm or this will affect the application and durability of the make-up. Increase ventilation as necessary.

9 Place all equipment and materials on the trolley or work surface in front of a make-up mirror.

10 Check the quality of the make-up sponges, if they have become crumbly following cleaning replace with new ones.

11 Collect the client's record card and put it on the treatment trolley.

12 Confirm that preparation of the work area meets with the Senior Therapist's satisfaction.

HEALTH AND SAFETY

Laundry
Dirty laundry should be placed in a covered container until cleaned.

Post treatment

Clean, tidy and prepare the work area in a suitable condition for further treatments.

- Dispose of the paper-tissue bedroll.
- Empty the bin that was used to collect waste in the treatment area. Replace the bin liner with a new one.
- Clean small bowls in hot, soapy water; rinse the bowls and dry.
- Clean the make-up brushes and make-up sponges in warm water and detergent; rinse thoroughly in clean water and allow them to dry naturally. Once dry, place in the ultraviolet cabinet. An alcohol-based cleaner can be used to clean brushes. The brushes are first cleaned as above. When dry they are briefly immersed in the alcohol solution and are then allowed to dry before placing in the ultraviolet cabinet.
- Clean the make-up palette in warm water and detergent, it might be necessary to remove stubborn marks with surgical spirit and clean cotton wool. Place in the ultraviolet cabinet.
- Ensure that the make-up products are clean, use a damp piece of cotton wool and surgical spirit to clean palettes and containers.
- Disinfect work surfaces.
- Protective towels and head-band, if used, should be removed from the treatment area and laundered.
- If a product needs to be disposed of, e.g. mascara, inform the relevant person for stock control before disposal and replacement. This will ensure adequate stock levels are maintained.
- Return the client record card to the secure storage area for client data.

PREPARING AND MAINTAINING THE BEAUTY THERAPY WORK AREA FOR MANICURE OR PEDICURE TREATMENT

Manicure and pedicures are treatments applied to the hands and feet:

- Manicure is a treatment to improve the appearance and condition of the hands, nails and skin

A client receiving a manicure

- Pedicure is a treatment to improve the appearance and condition of the feet, nail and skin.

A client receiving a pedicure

In addition to the manicure, specialist therapeutic treatments may be applied. These include:

- **Paraffin wax treatment**, a heat therapy treatment in which the hand or foot has heated liquid paraffin wax applied. This creates a heat-maintaining barrier for the skin. It takes approximately 20 minutes for the wax to melt to the correct consistency.

Paraffin wax treatment
Beauty Express

- **Thermal booties**, insulated boots for the feet are electrically heated to aid the absorption of treatment products for the skin of the feet.

Thermal booties   Ellisons

- **Thermal mitts**, insulated gloves for the hands are electrically heated to aid the absorption of treatment products for the skin of the hands.

Thermal mitts   Ellisons

- **Exfoliator cream** can be applied to remove dead skin and soften the skin. The skin appears brighter after treatment.

Manual exfoliation   Creative Nails

- **Treatment masks**, selected to stimulate, rejuvenate or nourish the skin. The hands can be placed in thermal mitts to intensify the effects achieved.

Treatment mask   Creative Nails

- **Warm oil**, oil is gently heated and applied to soften the skin and cuticles.

Warm oil heater   Ellisons

Pretreatment

Refer to the equipment and materials checklist to make sure that you have all that is required for manicure or pedicure treatment.

EQUIPMENT AND MATERIALS CHECKLIST FOR MANICURE/PEDICURE TREATMENT

	MANICURE	PEDICURE
Manicure/pedicure table or trolley	☐	☐
Medium-sized towels: three for manicure, five for pedicure	☐	☐
Small bowls lined with tissues (3) for clean cotton wool	☐	☐
Dry cotton wool to apply and remove products	☐	☐
Finger bowl for the client's fingers – to cleanse and soften the skin in warm water	☐	
Foot bowl or spa for the client's feet – to cleanse and soften the skin in warm water		☐
Emery board to file the nails to shape	☐	☐
Orange sticks, tipped at either end with cotton wool, to apply products to the nails and to clean the nail	☐	☐
Spatulas to remove products hygienically from their containers	☐	☐
Cuticle knife to remove skin from the nail	☐	☐
Hoof stick to push back the skin (the cuticle) around the bottom of the nail	☐	☐
Cuticle nippers to remove and neaten the appearance of excess cuticle	☐	☐
Nails scissors used to reduce the length of the nails	☐	
Toenail clippers to shorten the length of the toenails		☐
Buffers to give the nail a sheen and to increase blood circulation to the nail	☐	
Buffing paste, a coarse gritty nail product used to shine the nail plate when used with the buffer.	☐	
Detergent, to add to the warm water in the finger bowl or foot spa to cleanse and refresh the skin	☐	☐
Callus file to remove excess skin from the feet		☐
Hand cream, oil or lotion to soften and nourish the skin	☐	

Ellisons
Ellisons
Ellisons
Ellisons
Ellisons
Ellisons
Creative Nails

EQUIPMENT AND MATERIALS CHECKLIST FOR MANICURE/PEDICURE TREATMENT

	MANICURE	PEDICURE
Foot cream, oil or lotion to soften and nourish the skin		☐
Skin disinfectant to cleanse the skin before treatment	☐	☐
Base coat polish to provide a base to apply coloured polish and to prevent nail staining	☐	☐
Coloured polishes, a selection	☐	☐
Top coat to seal and protect nail polish colour providing durability	☐	☐
Specialist nail treatment products such as nail strengthener	☐	☐
Nail polish remover, to remove nail polish from the nail	☐	☐
Cuticle remover to soften the skin of the cuticle and to aid its removal	☐	☐
Cuticle oil to soften and nourish the skin of the cuticle	☐	☐
Cuticle massage cream to soften and nourish the skin of the cuticle	☐	☐
Jar of disinfecting solution to hold small metal and plastic manicure/pedicure tools	☐	☐
Paraffin wax treatment, specialist skin and nail treatment	☐	☐
Thermal booties, specialist skin and nail treatment		☐
Thermal mitts, specialist skin and nail treatment	☐	
Exfoliator cream to remove dead skin cells from the treatment area	☐	☐
Treatment masks, specialist skin treatment	☐	☐
Warm oil treatment, specialist skin and nail treatment	☐	
Plastic bags or plastic film to wrap the hands after the application of a heat or treatment mask	☐	☐
Bin (swing-top) – lined with a disposable polythene bin liner	☐	☐
Client's record card – to record the client's details before and after treatment	☐	☐
Aftercare leaflets to provide guidance on how to care for the nails, hands/feet after treatment	☐	☐

Creative Nail

Ellisons

Salon System

Jessica Nails

Salon System

Salon System

Creative Nail

Ellisons

Salon System

Ellisons

Sterilisation and disinfection

- Ensure tools and equipment are clean and sterile before use.
- Small metal tools should be sterilised after use. Clean them with surgical spirit and clean cotton wool and then sterilise them in the autoclave.
- Several sets of manicure/pedicure tools are required to ensure that time is allowed for disinfection/sterilisation after each treatment.
- Orange wood sticks, emery boards should be disposable and thrown away after use.
- Towels should be boil washed to destroy harmful micro-organisms and prevent cross-infection.
- Wash your hands before handling clean equipment.

Preparing the work area

1 The area should be clean and tidy.

2 There should be a clean, covered empty bin in the treatment area lined with a polythene bin liner.

3 Disinfect all work surfaces and cover with clean disposable paper tissue.

4 Check the trolley to make sure it has everything necessary to carry out the treatment.

5 Check whether a heat therapy treatment is to be applied. If using warm paraffin wax, make sure there is sufficient wax in the heater. Adjust the temperature according to manufacturer's instructions. Warm oil in the heater, following the manufacturer's instructions.

HEALTH AND SAFETY

Use of electrical equipment
Place equipment on a stable trolley and make sure that the wires do not trail or are in such a position that they might cause an accident.

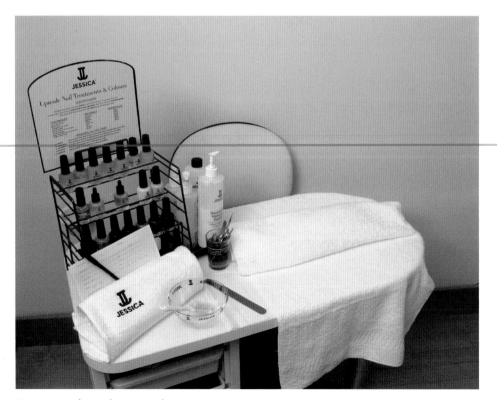

A prepared manicure station

6　Collect the small metal/plastic manicure/pedicure tools from the ultraviolet cabinet and place them in the jar of disinfecting solution.

7　Put all materials neatly onto the trolley.

8　A small table light might be needed for additional light when performing manicure treatment.

9　For **manicure**, place a towel over the work surface, then fold another towel into a pad and place it in the middle of the work surface. The pad supports the client's forearm during treatment. Place a third towel over the pad. Position a chair on either side of the manicure station, one for the client the other for the beauty therapist. Fill the finger bowl with warm water and detergent. Place a tissue or disposable manicure mat on top of the towels.

10　For **pedicure**, place a towel on the floor in between the therapist and client. Fill the foot bowl with warm water and detergent and put it on this towel. Five towels are required: one for the beauty therapist to place on her lap for protection, another should be provided to dry the client's feet, the other two are used to wrap the client's feet to keep them warm during pedicure treatment.

11　Collect the client's record card and put it on the treatment trolley.

12　Confirm the preparation of the work area meets with the Senior Therapist's satisfaction.

Post treatment

Clean, tidy and prepare the work area in a suitable condition for further treatments.

- Dispose of the paper-tissue bedroll and other disposable items such as emery boards, spatulas and orange sticks.
- Empty the bin that was used to collect waste in the treatment area. Replace the bin liner with a new one.
- Clean small bowls in hot, soapy water; rinse and dry.
- Clean all tools and metal equipment with surgical spirit and sterilise in the autoclave.
- Plastic equipment should be cleaned in hot soapy water, dried and placed in the ultraviolet cabinet.
- Dispose of the brushes used to apply paraffin wax; they cannot be cleaned.
- The buffer, if used, should have the chamois leather cover cleaned in warm soapy water at 60°C. When dried, it should be sanitised in the ultraviolet cabinet. The plastic handle should be wiped with surgical spirit.
- Clean mask brushes in hot, soapy water, dry and put in the ultraviolet cabinet.
- Electrical equipment should be cleaned to remove any spillage. Switch off equipment before cleaning and use specialist equipment cleaner to clean. If the equipment is to be used again, switch on after cleaning. Replenish products as necessary.
- Clean the necks of bottles and jars to maintain hygiene and a high standard

of presentation. Nail polish bottle necks should be cleaned regularly with clean cotton wool and nail polish remover to ensure that they close tightly or the polish will become thick in consistency.

- Disinfect work surfaces.
- Remove used towels from the treatment area and launder them.
- If a product needs to be disposed of, e.g. a nail polish, inform the relevant person for stock control before disposal and replacement. This will ensure adequare stock levels are maintained.
- Return the client record card to the secure storage area for client data.

PREPARING AND MAINTAINING THE BEAUTY THERAPY WORK AREA FOR FACIAL TREATMENT

A facial is a treatment applied to the skin of the face that has a cleansing, toning, nourishing effect of the skin.

Sterilisation and disinfection

- Ensure tools and equipment are clean and sterile before use.
- Several sets of facial sponges and mask brushes will be required to ensure that time is allowed for disinfection/sterilisation after each treatment.
- Towels and head bands should be boil washed to destroy harmful micro-organisms and prevent cross-infection.

A client receiving a facial treatment

● Wash your hands before handling clean equipment.

Pretreatment

EQUIPMENT AND MATERIALS CHECKLIST FOR FACIAL TREATMENT

Couch or beauty chair with sit-up and lie-down positions and an easy-to-clean surface ☐

Trolley to hold all the necessary equipment and materials ☐

Large and medium-sized towels to protect the client's clothing and for the beauty therapist to dry their hands during treatment
Note: The client could be offered a gown to wear: place a clean gown in the treatment area. ☐

Disposable tissue roll to cover the trolley surface ☐

Head-band to protect the client's hair and to keep hair away from the treatment area ☐

Dampened, clean cotton wool, to remove skin-care products ☐

Cotton wool eye pads preshaped round and dampened to place over the eyes during the mask treatment.
Note: Two further cotton wool eye pads will be required if facial steaming is being carried out to protect the delicate eye tissue. ☐

Facial tissues to blot the skin dry after toner and following mask removal ☐

Small bowls to store damp and dry cotton wool, mix treatment masks, hold cosmetic creams that have been dispensed ☐

Spatulas to remove products hygienically from containers and to tuck the client hair underneath the head-band to prevent soiling. ☐

Non-oily eye make-up remover to cleanse the eye area (to prevent the make-up being a barrier to treatment) ☐

Cleansing lotion – a range available to suit the different skin types
Normal, dry, combination, oily, sensitive ☐

Toning lotion – a range available to suit the different skin types
Normal, dry, combination, oily, sensitive ☐

EQUIPMENT AND MATERIALS CHECKLIST FOR FACIAL TREATMENT

Elemis

Moisturiser – a range available to suit the different skin types
Normal, dry, combination, oily, sensitive ☐

Mask brush to apply facial masks ☐

Sorisa

Massage oil/cream ☐

Magnifier lamp (cold) to enlarge the appearance of the treatment area ☐

Skin warming device:
facial steamer vapour unit ☐
towel steaming ☐

Ellisons

Distilled water to fill the tank of the vapour unit ☐
Note: Consult the senior beauty therapist to see if she is using a skin warming device in her treatment.

Elemis

Skin exfoliation product, to remove the surface dead skin cells
exposing fresh new cells. ☐

Specialist skin products: ☐
eye creams   eye gels
lip balms   neck creams   acne products

Ellisons

Setting masks, which absorb dead skin, the skin's natural oil (sebum)
and debris – usually to cleanse and improve the skin tone. ☐
Note: Some masks require other ingredients to be added. Check what
is required for the mask treatment with the senior beauty therapist
when preparing the work area.

Silhouette-Dermalift Silhouette-Dermalift

Non-setting masks containing emollients – skin softening ingredients
that soften and nourish the skin ☐

Mask removal sponges. Large, high-quality cotton wool discs
can be used in preference to sponges. (Sponges are preferable for use on
male clients) ☐
Note: If a sink is not available for the beauty therapist, a large bowl
will be required filled with warm water to remove the mask.

Ellisons

Mirror (clean) to show the client the skin after treatment ☐

Ellisons

Bin (swing-top) lined with a disposable bin liner ☐

Client record card – to record client's personal details before and
after treatment ☐

Ellisons

After care leaflets to provide guidance on how to care for the skin
after treatment ☐

Refer to the equipment and materials checklist to make sure that you have all that is required for facial treatment.

Preparing the treatment area

1 The area should be clean and tidy.

2 There should be a clean, covered empty bin lined with a polythene bin liner.

3 Disinfect all work surfaces and cover with clean disposable paper tissue.

4 Check the trolley to make sure it contains everything needed to carry out the treatment.

5 Collect facial equipment from the ultraviolet cabinet, mask brush and mask removal sponges and place on the trolley.

6 Prepare cotton wool: provide a selection of damp and dry cotton wool placed on the trolley, usually in small bowls.

7 The beauty couch or chair should be protected with a long strip of disposable bedroll or a freshly laundered sheet and bath towel.

8 Adjust the lighting – the room should be gently lit for facial treatment, to induce relaxation.

9 Check that the magnifying lamp is clean and in good working area.

10 Check the room temperature, good ventilation is important – it should not be too warm.

11 A large towel should be provided to cover the client's body and a small towel to drape across the client's chest and shoulders. Place these neatly on the treatment couch.

A towel warmer   Ellisons

A facial steamer vapour unit
Sonisa

A prepared facial trolley

12 A clean gown can be provided, if the client prefers, to wear after removing outer clothing (a requirement if the client is receiving facial massage to the chest and shoulders).

13 If a skin-warming device is to be used, this should be prepared ready for use:

   a Hot towels: clean, sterile towels should be placed in the towel warmer. Follow the manufacturer's guidelines for heating timings.

   b Facial steamer vapour unit: fill the water tank with distilled water up to the maximum level. Switch on the machine at the mains, select the steam facility and heat the water until steam can be seen. Switch off the unit. This will save time as the water will now only need to be reheated.

14 Collect the client's record card and place on the treatment trolley.

15 Confirm the preparation of the work area meets with the Senior Therapist's satisfaction.

Post treatment

Clean, tidy and prepare the work area in a suitable condition for further treatments.

- Dispose of the paper-tissue bedroll.
- Empty the bin that was used to collect waste in the treatment areas. Replace the bin liner with a new one.
- Disinfect work surfaces.
- Clean bowls used in hot soapy water, rinse and dry.
- Clean the mask brushes in warm water and detergent, rinse thoroughly in clean water and allow them to dry naturally. Once dry, place them in the ultraviolet cabinet.
- Wash the mask-removal sponges in warm water and detergent and then sterilise in the autoclave. Place in the ultraviolet cabinet when dry, ready for use.
- Ensure the facial steamer, if used, is switched off and disconnected at the mains. Check the water level and refill with distilled water ready for future use.
- Used towels, including facial towels used to warm the skin, the head-band and gown (if worn) should be removed from the treatment area and laundered.
- If a product needs to be disposed of, e.g. a facial mask, inform the relevant person for stock control before disposal and replacement. This will ensure adequare stock levels are maintained.
- Return the client record card to the secure storage area for client data.

Glossary

Cross-infection	the transfer of contagious micro-organisms
Data Protection Act (1998)	legislation designed to protect client privacy and confidentiality
Disinfection	the destruction of some, but not all micro-organisms
Environmental conditions	the surroundings in which the treatment will be performed
Eyebrow-shaping treatment	removal of brow hair to maintain or create a new shape
Eyelash-perming treatment	the use of chemical lotions to permanently curl the lash hair
Eye treatments	treatments applied to the eye area to enhance the appearance of the eye
Eyelash and eyebrow tinting treatment	the permanent colouring of the lash and/or brow hair using a specialist dye to enhance their appearance
Facial	a treatment applied to the skin of the face; it has a skin cleansing, toning and nourishing effect
False lash treatment	threads of artificial hair attached to the natural lashes to make them appear thicker and longer
Hygiene	the recommended standard of cleanliness necessary in the salon to prevent cross-infection
Legislation	laws that affect the beauty therapy business and which relate to products and services, the business premises and environmental conditions, working practices and those employed
Maintain	to keep
Make-up treatment	the application of make-up cosmetics to enhance the skin and facial features
Manicure treatment	a treatment to improve the appearance of the hands, nails and skin
Pedicure treatment	a treatment to improve the appearance of the feet, nails and skin
Personal Protective Equipment (PPE) at Work Regs (1992)	legislation that requires employers to identify, through risk assessment, those activities that require special protective equipment to be worn
Post (treatment)	later (what to do after treatment)
Preparation	to get ready
Record card	personal information recorded for each client, also recording treatments received and retail product purchases
Sterilisation	the destruction of all micro-organisms
Waxing	the use of wax to remove hairs temporarily from the face and body

Assessment of knowledge and understanding

Unit BT1: Prepare and maintain the beauty therapy work area

You have now learned how to prepare and maintain the beauty therapy work area for waxing, eye treatments, manicure, pedicure and facial treatments. The skills developed enable you to professionally prepare and maintain the beauty therapy work area. To test your level of knowledge and understanding, answer the following short questions, these will prepare you for your summative (final) assessment.

Preparing the beauty therapy work area

1 Why is it important to keep accurate client records?

2 Why is it important that you wash your hands before preparing the work area?

3 Why is it important to follow the senior therapist's instructions for preparing the work area?

4 How can cross-infection be avoided when preparing the work area?

5 How can you ensure your own personal hygiene? Give three examples.

6 Define the terms:
   a sterilisation
   b disinfection

7 Name a piece of equipment used in sterilising beauty therapy equipment.

8 Name a piece of equipment used to disinfect beauty therapy equipment.

9 What chemicals are used for disinfecting?

10 Why must you check the environmental conditions when preparing the work area for: heating, lighting and ventilation?

Maintaining the beauty therapy work area

1 How should wax waste be disposed of?

2 Why should the manufacturer's instructions be followed when using treatment materials and equipment?

3 Why should you know the storage requirements for different products?

4 Why should you regularly check the appointment book when planning your time to prepare and maintain the work areas for different treatments?

5 Where should the client's records be stored after treatment?

6 How should you aim to leave the treatment area after treatment?

7 How would you clean the following:
   a metal manicure tools
   b make-up brushes
   c wax heater
   d eyelash tinting bowls
   e facial mask brush and sponges

chapter 4

BT2 Assist with facial treatments

Learning objectives

This chapter covers the skills and knowledge you need to assist with facial treatments. It describes the competencies to enable you to:

- prepare for facial treatments

- carry out facial treatments

- complete the treatments.

When performing facial treatments, it is important to consider all health and safety requirements using the knowledge you gained from Unit G1: Ensure your own actions reduce risks to health and safety (see Chapter 1).

Client with facial mask applied Silhouette-Dermalift

PRACTICAL SKILLS AND KNOWLEDGE

The table shown here will help you to check your progress in gaining the necessary practical skills and knowledge for Unit BT2: Assist with facial treatments.

Tick (✓), when you feel you have gained your practical skills and knowledge in the following areas:

Practical skills and knowledge checklist	✓
1 The treatment aim of a basic facial treatment	
2 Contra-indications that prevent a facial treatment	
3 Equipment and products that are needed	
4 How to prepare the treatment area	
5 How to prepare yourself before the facial treatment	
6 Client consultation	
7 How to prepare the client	
8 How to carry out the basic facial treatment	
9 After-care and advice to be given to the client following treatment	
10 Contra-actions to look for during or following the facial treatment	

When you have ticked all the areas you can, ask your assessor to assess you on Unit BT2: Assist with facial treatments. After practical assessment, your assessor might decide that you need to practise further to improve your skills. If so, your assessor will tell you how and where you need to improve to gain competence.

FACIAL TREATMENTS

As well as looking after the skin from the inside, by diet, it needs care from the outside – it must be kept clean and it must be nourished.

When it is functioning normally, the skin becomes oily and sweat is deposited on its surface. The natural oil in the skin (called sebum) can easily build up on the skin's surface and block the natural openings – the pores – on the surface of the skin; this can lead to infection. Facial cosmetics also affect the health of the skin; if not regularly removed, they can cause blockages. Skin-care treatments help to maintain and improve the functioning of the skin.

The basic facial treatment aims to improve the overall appearance and condition of the skin by the application of appropriate skin-care treatments and products. The facial treatment includes:

- consultation and skin analysis
- skin cleansing
- skin toning
- the application of a face mask
- moisturiser application.

The skin varies in appearance, according to our race, sex and age. It alters from season to season, year to year and reflects our general health, lifestyle and diet. The functioning of the different parts of the skin gives us our **skin type**, e.g. dry, oily or combination.

ANATOMY AND PHYSIOLOGY OF THE SKIN

You need to know about the skin, its structure and function (how it works) so that you can improve its appearance and understand how to care for it properly.

Basic functions of the skin

The skin has many functions; the main functions are listed below.

Protection

The skin helps to protect the body from harmful substances and conditions, and cushions the underlying structures in the body from physical injury. The outer surface of the skin is bactericidal, which helps to prevent the growth of harmful micro-organisms. The tough, waterproof construction of the skin forms a barrier that prevents the absorption of many substances, and also prevents the skin losing vital water, which would cause it to dry out. Cells in the skin contain a pigment called melanin, which gives us our skin colour and absorbs harmful rays of ultraviolet light. The amount of melanin in the skin varies between individuals and between races.

Temperature control

Man has a normal body temperature maintained at 36.8–37°C.

Body temperature is controlled in part by heat loss through the skin and by sweating.

HEALTH AND SAFETY ✚

Allergic reactions
If the skin is allergic or is sensitive to something this shows as an allergic reaction. The skin becomes red, itchy and swollen. At the consultation you must check whether a client is allergic to anything so that you don't cause an allergic reaction.

Client with allergic reaction
Dr John Gray, *The World of Skin Care*

If the body temperature is increased by 0.25–0.5°C, the sweat glands secrete sweat to the skin's surface. The body is cooled by the loss of heat used to evaporate the sweat from the skin's surface.

If the body becomes too warm there is an increase in blood flow into the blood capillaries in the skin. The blood capillaries widen and heat is lost from the skin.

Sensitivity

The skin allows the feelings of **touch**, **pressure**, **heat** and **cold**, and allows us to recognise objects by their feel and shape. These are recognised by nerve endings in the skin called *sensory nerve endings*.

Basic structure of the skin

The skin is the largest organ in the body, accounting for one-eighth of the body's total weight. It is made up of microscopic cells, which provide a tough, flexible covering, and have many important functions. Each cell contains various specialised structures surrounded by a chemical substance called **protoplasm**. The activities of these cells are essential for our general health. If the cells cannot function properly, a disorder results.

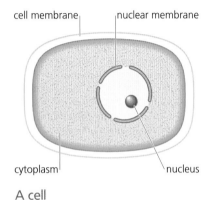

cell membrane | nuclear membrane
cytoplasm | nucleus

A cell

Each cell is surrounded by the **cell membrane**. This membrane is porous, allowing food to enter and waste materials to leave.

In the centre of the cell is the **nucleus**, which contains the **chromosomes** that carry the genes we have inherited from our parents. Genes are responsible for cell reproduction and functioning.

The liquid that surrounds the nucleus is called the cell **cytoplasm**.

If we used a microscope to look inside the skin we would be able to see two distinct layers: the **epidermis** (the top layer of the skin) and the **dermis**. Situated below the epidermis and the dermis is a further layer, the **subcutaneous layer** or **fat layer**.

epidermis
basement membrane
dermis
subcutaneous layer

The skin

The epidermis

The main function of the epidermis is to protect the deeper living structures in the body from invasion and harm by the external environment.

The epidermis lies directly above the dermis layer. It is composed of five layers, with the outer surface layer being the skin we can see and touch. This is the most significant layer of the skin with regard to the external application of skin-care products. Each layer of the epidermis can be recognised by the shape of its cells.

Over a period of about four weeks, cells move from the bottom layer of the epidermis to the top layer – the skin's surface – changing in shape and structure as they progress through the different layers.

The outer layer of the skin's epidermis shown with an electron microscope

Dr John Gray, *The World of Skin Care*

The process of cellular change

The cell is formed

↓

The cell matures
It changes in structure and moves upwards and outwards

↓

It moves upwards and becomes an empty shell which is shed

TIP ✓

Keratin
The main type of cell in the epidermis is the keratinocyte, which produces a substance called keratin. Keratin makes the skin tough and reduces the entry of substances into the skin. Keratin is the main substance that forms hair and nails.

The five layers of the epidermis are:

1 *stratum corneum* or cornified layer
2 *stratum lucidum* or clear layer or lucid layer
3 *stratum granulosum* or granular layer
4 *stratum mucosum or spinosum* or prickle-cell layer
5 *stratum germinativum* or basal layer.

Stratum corneum or cornified or horny layer

This outer layer is formed from several layers of flattened, scale-like overlapping cells, composed mainly of keratin. These help to reflect ultraviolet light from the skin's surface; darker skins can tolerate strong ultraviolet light and has a thicker stratum corneum than paler skins.

It takes about four weeks for the epidermal cells to reach the stratum corneum from the stratum germinativum. The cells are then shed in a process called **desquamation**.

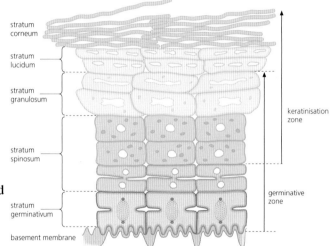

Layers of the epidermis

Stratum lucidum or clear layer or lucid layer

This layer is seen only in non-hairy areas of the skin such as the palms of the hands and soles of the feet. The cells here lack a nucleus and are filled with clear substances called *eledin*.

Stratum granulosum or granular layer

This is composed of two or three layers of flattish cells. The nucleus of the cell has begun to break up, creating granules within the cell cytoplasm. These granules later form keratin.

Stratum mucosum or spinosum or prickle-cell layer

The stratum spinosum or prickle-cell layer is formed from between two and six rows of cells that have a surface of spiky spines, which connect to surrounding cells. Each cell has a large nucleus filled with fluid.

TIP ✓

Removing dead cells
When we cleanse the skin and apply specialist skin products, such as a treatment mask, we remove dead cells from the surface of the epidermis.
Every five days we shed a complete surface layer.

Collagen and elastin fibres
Hugh Rushton

Aged skin   Dr John Gray, *The World of Skin Care*

TIP ✓

Blood supply
When you massage the skin's surface when applying cleansing products, you increase the blood supply to the skin and so assist the removal of waste products from the skin. This improves the health and functioning of the skin.

Stratum germinativum or basal layer

This is the deepest layer of the epidermis. It is formed from a single layer of column-shaped cells. These cells divide continuously and produce new cells. Melanocytes are found in this layer; these cells produce the skin pigment *melanin* and give the skin its colour.

The dermis

The dermis is the inner part of the skin underneath the epidermis. It is much thicker than the epidermis and contains a network of fibres that give skin its strength and elasticity. There are two types of fibres:

- yellow elastin gives the skin its elasticity
- white collagen gives the skin its strength.

As the skin begins to age this network loses strength and elasticity, resulting in facial lines and slack skin.

The dermis also contains other structures such as blood vessels, lymph vessels and nerves.

There are different types of nerve ending, which sense touch, pressure and temperature. They inform us about the outside world and what is happening on the skin's surface. They are more numerous in sensitive parts of the skin such as the lips and the fingertips.

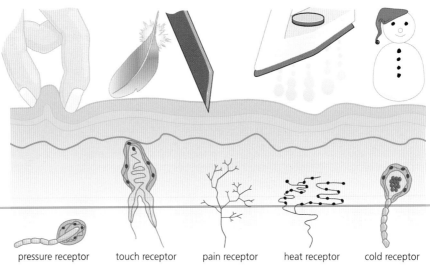

pressure receptor   touch receptor   pain receptor   heat receptor   cold receptor

Sensory nerves

Near the surface of the dermis are tiny projections called *papillae*. These contain nerve endings and blood capillaries which supply the upper epidermis with nutrition.

The blood supply to the skin

Nutrients and oxygen, which are essential for the skin's health and growth, are brought to the dermis in the blood. The blood vessels that bring blood to the dermis also take away some waste products. Other waste products (e.g. used blood cells) are carried away by the lymph vessels.

Skin appendages

Within the dermis are structures called skin appendages. These include:

- sweat glands
- hair follicles, which produce hair
- sebaceous glands
- nails.

Sweat glands   These are small tubes in the skin, extending from the epidermis into the dermis. They are found all over the body, especially on the soles of the feet and palms of the hands. The main function of the sweat glands is to control body temperature. Sweat, a fluid, flows onto the skin's surface through a sweat pore and evaporates, creating a cooling effect. We each have 2–5 million sweat glands.

Pores allow the absorption of some facial products into the skin. The facial treatment is aimed at cleansing the pores with facial cleansers and masks.

The pores may become enlarged because of blockages caused by dirt, dead skin cells and cosmetics. The application of toning lotion creates a skin tightening effect upon the skin's surface, slightly reducing the size of the pores.

Hair follicles   These are downward tube-like growths in the epidermis and dermis of the skin. They are found all over the body except on the palms of the hands and soles of the feet. At the bottom of each follicle is a cluster of cells that divide and move up the hair follicle, changing in structure and forming a **hair**.

A sweat gland

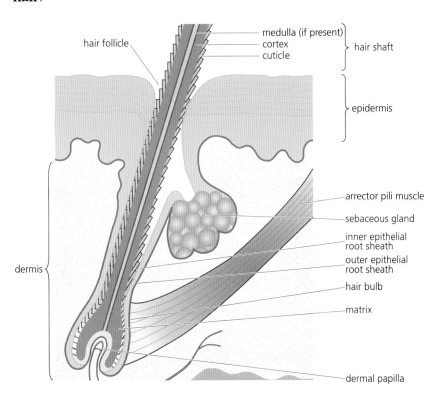

Cross-section of the skin, hair and hair follicle

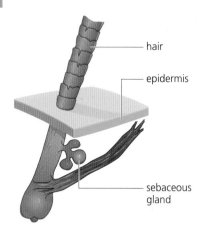

hair

epidermis

sebaceous gland

A sebaceous gland

Sebaceous glands   These are minute sac-like organs. They are found all over the body, except the palms of the hands and soles of the feet. The cells of the gland break down and form an oil called **sebum**. The activity of the sebaceous gland is increased at puberty, when stimulated by a chemical messenger carried in the blood called a hormone. In adults, the activity slows down again. Men secrete slightly more sebum than women.

Sebum has bactericidal and fungicidal properties, which help discourage the growth of harmful micro-organisms on the skin surface, which could lead to skin disease. Sebum also prevents loss of moisture from the surface of the skin.

Cosmetic moisturisers mimic sebum in providing an oily covering for the skin's surface to reduce moisture loss.

The acid mantle

Sweat and sebum combine on the skin surface to create an acid film called the acid mantle. This discourages the growth of bacteria and fungi.

HEALTH AND SAFETY	

Protecting the skin's acid mantle
Some products that come into contact with the skin (such as some soaps) are alkaline, and can destroy the skin's acid mantle. If these products are used on the skin, the acid mantle will take several hours to restore itself and the skin might become irritated, reddened and sensitive.

TIP	✓

Sebum and skin types
An overactive sebaceous gland produces a large amount of sebum and results in an 'oily' skin type.
If the sebaceous gland is underactive, it produces less sebum and the skin is termed 'dry'.

SKIN TYPES

How the skin functions and how we care for it give us our skin type. The basic skin types that you need to be able to recognise and treat are:

- oily (also known as greasy)
- dry
- combination.

A skin analysis – an inspection of the client's skin – helps us to identify skin type.

How to recognise different skin types

Oily skin

The sebaceous glands are very active, especially at puberty (sexual maturity). An increase in sebum production often causes the appearance of skin blemishes. Sebaceous gland activity begins to decrease in a person's twenties.

Oily skin:

- has large pores
- has a coarse texture (not smooth)

Oily skin   Dr John Gray, *The World of Skin Care*

- appears thick
- is usually sallow (a yellowy colour) as a result of excess sebum production
- appears shiny due to excess sebum production
- possesses good skin strength (tone) because of the protective effect of sebum
- might show certain skin disorders, e.g. comedones (blackheads), pustules and papules (blemishes caused by bacterial infection of the skin).

Dry skin

Dry skin is lacking in sebum, moisture or both. Because sebum limits the loss of moisture from the skin's surface, skin with insufficient sebum loses moisture more quickly becoming **dehydrated**. A dehydrated skin is one that has lost waster from its tissues. A dry skin:

- has small tight pores
- has poor moisture content
- has a thin, coarse texture
- often exhibits patches of flaking skin
- often has sensitive areas, showing broken capillaries as a result of reduced sebum protection
- might contain milia (sebaceous blockages, accumulated in the hair follicle) – small, hard, pearly white cysts that are often seen around the eye area.

Combination skin

This skin is partly dry and partly oily. The oily parts are generally the chin, nose and forehead known as the **T-zone**. The upper cheeks might also show signs of oiliness but the rest of the face and neck is dry. In a combination skin:

- there are enlarged pores in the T-zone and small to medium-sized pores in the cheek area
- the moisture content is high in the oily areas but poor in the dry areas
- the skin is coarse and thick in the oily areas but thinner in the dry areas
- the skin is sallow on the oily areas but shows sensitivity in the dry areas
- the skin tone is good in the oily areas but poor in the dry areas
- there may be blemishes such as pustules and comedones at the T-zone
- milia and broken capillaries might appear in the dry areas, commonly on the cheeks and near the eyes.

Allergic skin

Allergic skin is irritated by external **allergens** – substances that cause sensitivity. The allergens inflame the skin and might damage its protective function. At the consultation, always check whether the client has any allergies, and if so what.

Contact with an allergen, especially if repeated, can cause skin disorders such as eczema and dermatitis. If a skin is sensitive, use hypo-allergenic products – those that do not contain any of the known allergens.

Dry skin   Dr John Gray, *The World of Skin Care*

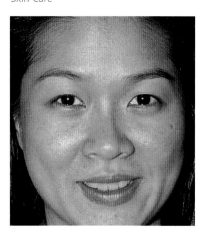

Combination skin   Dr John Gray, *The World of Skin Care*

ACTIVITY

Recognising skin types
Refer to the illustration below. What skin characteristics would you expect to see in each of the numbered areas? Consider each of the skin types discussed.

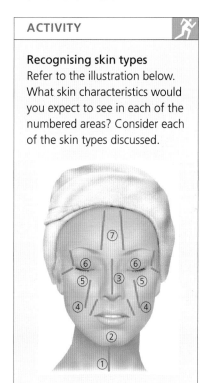

STEP BY STEP: BASIC FACIAL TREATMENT

1 Consultation Silhouette-Dermalift

2 Skin analysis

3 Eye make-up removal

4 Superficial cleanse Silhouette-Dermalift

5 Deep cleanse Silhouette-Dermalift

6 Skin toning Silhouette-Dermalift

7 Mask application Silhouette-Dermalift

8 Mask removal (setting mask)
Silhouette-Dermalift

9 Skin toning Silhouette-Dermalift

ACTIVITY

Timing
What is the time allowed for a
basic facial treatment?
Why is it important to complete
the treatment in this time?
Think of three reasons for each.

10 Skin moisturising   Silhouette-Dermalift

Making the appointment

When a client makes an appointment for a basic facial treatment, the receptionist should ask a few basic questions:

- What is the client's name and telephone number? This will help you to get the client record card ready before they arrive for treatment. The telephone number is important in case you need to cancel the treatment for any reason, e.g. the beauty therapist is ill.
- Which therapist does the client want to see? If a particular therapist is needed you will have to check on availability.
- When does the client want the treatment, i.e. day/date and time? If any of these are not available, suggest another time or day as near to this as possible.
- Has the client had the treatment before? This allows the client to ask you questions about the treatment.
- Does the client require any other services in addition to the basic facial treatment? Always look at opportunities to increase treatment bookings: the salon needs to keep busy!

Remember, when making an appointment it is important to allow enough time to complete the treatment properly. It is also important for the therapist to be able to complete the treatment in a commercially acceptable time. Allow 45 minutes for a basic facial treatment.

The Data Protection Act (1998)

These details are confidential, or private. All information relating to a client should be stored securely. Only those staff with permission to access it can do so. Therefore, as soon as all treatment details have been recorded on the record card, the client's details should be stored securely. It is important that all details are accurate and up to date.

Before treatment

Before treatment is carried out you will need to prepare the work area, yourself and client for the treatment.

Outcome 1: Prepare for facial treatments

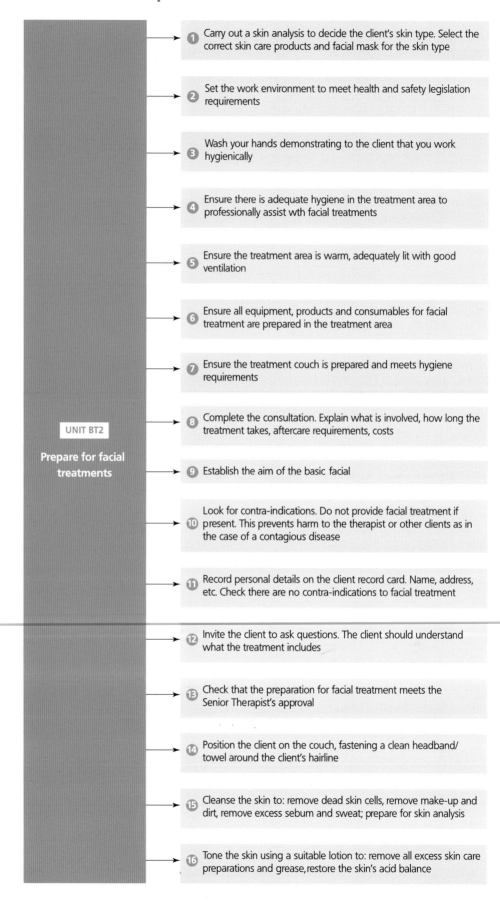

UNIT BT2

Prepare for facial treatments

1. Carry out a skin analysis to decide the client's skin type. Select the correct skin care products and facial mask for the skin type

2. Set the work environment to meet health and safety legislation requirements

3. Wash your hands demonstrating to the client that you work hygienically

4. Ensure there is adequate hygiene in the treatment area to professionally assist wth facial treatments

5. Ensure the treatment area is warm, adequately lit with good ventilation

6. Ensure all equipment, products and consumables for facial treatment are prepared in the treatment area

7. Ensure the treatment couch is prepared and meets hygiene requirements

8. Complete the consultation. Explain what is involved, how long the treatment takes, aftercare requirements, costs

9. Establish the aim of the basic facial

10. Look for contra-indications. Do not provide facial treatment if present. This prevents harm to the therapist or other clients as in the case of a contagious disease

11. Record personal details on the client record card. Name, address, etc. Check there are no contra-indications to facial treatment

12. Invite the client to ask questions. The client should understand what the treatment includes

13. Check that the preparation for facial treatment meets the Senior Therapist's approval

14. Position the client on the couch, fastening a clean headband/towel around the client's hairline

15. Cleanse the skin to: remove dead skin cells, remove make-up and dirt, remove excess sebum and sweat; prepare for skin analysis

16. Tone the skin using a suitable lotion to: remove all excess skin care preparations and grease, restore the skin's acid balance

Contra-indications to treatment

Certain skin and eye conditions prevent you from performing the basic facial treatment, these are known as **contra-indications**.

If, when looking at the client's skin and eyes before the treatment, you think you recognise any of the following conditions, basic facial treatment must not be carried out. You will need to refer the client tactfully to the relevant person in the salon to get confirmation as to whether the treatment can go ahead.

Conditions that prevent treatment

All the skin and eye conditions listed below are contagious – they can be passed to other clients. You must never treat a client with any of these conditions.

Name of contra-indication	Cause	Appearance
Impetigo	A contagious **bacterial** infection caused by minute, single-celled organisms and which results in skin inflammation	The skin appears red and is itchy. Small blisters appear, which burst and then form crusts
Tinea Corporis or **body ringworm**	A contagious **fungal** infection of the skin. Fungal diseases of the skin feed off the waste products of the skin	Small, scaly red patches spread outwards and then heal from the centre, leaving a ring. Found on the limbs
Conjunctivitis or **pink eye**	A contagious **bacterial** infection of the mucous membrane that covers the eyelids	The skin of the inner conjunctiva of the eye becomes inflamed, the eye becomes very red and sore, and pus might appear
Hordeola or **styes**	A contagious **bacterial** infection of the sebaceous glands of eyelash hair follicles	Small lumps appear, usually containing pus at the skin around the base of the eyelash hair
Furuncles or **boils**	A contagious **bacterial** infection in the skin around the hair follicle	Red, painful lumps extend into the skin around a hair follicle. A core of pus develops
Herpes simplex or **cold sore**	A contagious **viral** disorder of the skin. Viruses require living tissue to survive. They invade the healthy cell and multiply within the cell. Cold sores often appear when skin's resistance is low due to stress or ill health	Inflammation of the skin occurs in localised areas. The skin becomes red and feels itchy, and small blisters appear. These are followed by a crust, which might crack and weep tissue fluid

Dr M H Beck

HEALTH AND SAFETY

Contra-indication
Remember – you might be wrong when you think you have a client with a contra-indication.

Always check with the Senior Therapist if unsure – the client might be able to have the treatment after all.

Never diagnose and try to avoid causing the client embarrassment.

The Senior Therapist may recommend that the client seeks medical advice before facial treatment goes ahead.

HEALTH AND SAFETY

Cold sores
Clients who suffer from cold sores (herpes simplex) should avoid ultraviolet light because this can stimulate production of the sores.

Conditions that might restrict treatment

The skin conditions below are non-contagious – they cannot be passed to other clients. Clients with these conditions can be treated, but you might need to adapt your treatment application.

Name of contra-indication	Cause	Appearance	Treatment
Skin eczema Dr M H Beck	Inflammation of the skin caused by contact with a skin irritant	The skin becomes red, swells and blisters can appear. The blisters burst, which causes scabs to form on the skin	Ensure you find out what irritants make the eczema worse and avoid contact with such products, e.g. it might be perfumed products. The skin can benefit from cosmetic products that contain soothing ingredients such as lavender. Do not treat if the skin is broken
Skin psoriasis Dr M H Beck	Cause unknown but becomes worse when the person is stressed. Often hereditary	Itchy, red, flaky patches of skin, which can become infected if the skin is broken	The skin can benefit from cosmetic products that contain soothing ingredients such as lavender. Do not treat if the skin is broken
Broken bones	Injury – should be treated medically	The breakage might not be obvious. Therefore, if the client is new, check there have been no recent broken bones at the consultation	The broken bone must not be handled. Always check first with the relevant person in the workplace

---

HEALTH AND SAFETY

Skin disorders
If a client shows a skin disorder and you are at all unsure, check with the relevant person in the workplace before starting treatment.
A client with a skin disorder is usually advised to visit their GP. This is relevant for all contra-indications that prohibit treatment and also for those that restrict treatment, mainly eczema and psoriasis.

HEALTH AND SAFETY

Cuts, abrasions, bruising, redness and swelling
If the skin has been damaged but is no longer infected or at risk from secondary infection, you might be able to treat the skin. Check with the senior beauty therapist before you proceed.

Equipment and materials

Before carrying out the basic facial, check that you have all the necessary equipment and materials at hand. Refer to the equipment and materials checklist to make sure that you have all that is required to perform a basic facial treatment. Tick next to each item on the checklist to help you as you prepare the work area.

EQUIPMENT, MATERIALS AND PRODUCTS CHECKLIST

Sorisa	Treatment couch or beauty chair
Sorisa	Equipment trolley on which to place everything required for the facial treatment
Sorisa	Beauty stool; for the comfort of the beauty therapist this should have a back rest and be adjustable in height, to allow mobility
Sorisa	Magnifying lamp (cold) – floor standing or trolley mounted – to enlarge the surface appearance of the skin when performing the skin analysis
Ellisons	Small bowls lined with tissues (3): one for the client's jewellery and two for clean, dry and damp cotton wool, plus a large bowl to hold warm water during removal of the mask if a sink is not available in the treatment area
Salon Systems	Facial skin cleansing preparations to suit all skin types, including eye make-up remover, cleanser, toner and moisturiser – choose a skin cleansing preparation that contains a variety of different ingredients to achieve a deep cleansing, toning, nourishing or refreshing effect upon the skin according to skin type
Ellisons	Mask brush – disinfected for each client – to apply the mask to the skin of the face and neck
Silhouette-Dermalift	Sterilised mask removal sponges (2) for removing the mask in warm water
Ellisons	Headband

Sorisa

Towels (2) – freshly laundered for each client. A large towel should cover the client's body and a small hand towel should be draped across the client's chest and shoulders, plus an extra clean towel for the therapist to use as necessary

☐

Ellisons

A clean gown for each client as necessary

☐

Ellisons

A plentiful supply of damp and dry cotton wool – sufficient for the treatment to be carried out

☐

Sorisa

Cotton buds to cleanse excess make-up left along the lash line following eye cleansing

☐

Sorisa

Facial tissues should be large and of a high quality. They should be stored in a covered container

☐

Hand mirror (clean) for consulting with the client before and after treatment

☐

Ellisons

Several clean spatulas (preferably disposable) for each client. One should be used to tuck any stray hair beneath the head-band; others will be used to remove products from their containers

☐

Ellisons

Lined swing waste bin to collect waste materials during and following treatment. Place unobtrusively within easy reach.

☐

Ellisons

Client's record card to record all personal details and record details of the treatment

☐

Ellisons

Disinfecting solution to keep the small tools hygienic once sterilised

☐

Client record card and treatment plan details for you to complete before, during and following treatment

BEAUTY WORKS

Date	Therapist name	
Client name		Date of birth (identifying client age group)
Address		Postcode

Evening phone number   Day phone number

Name of doctor   Doctor's address and phone number

Related medical history (conditions that may restrict or prohibit treatment application)

Are you taking any medication? (this may affect the appearance of the skin or skin sensitivity)

CONTRA-INDICATIONS REQUIRING MEDICAL REFERRAL
(Preventing **facial treatment** application)

☐ bacterial infections (e.g. impetigo)
☐ viral infections (e.g. herpes simplex)
☐ fungal infections (e.g. tinea ungium)
☐ eye infections (e.g. conjunctivitis)
☐ systemic medical conditions
☐ severe skin conditions

SKIN GROUP

☐ oily   ☐ dry   ☐ combination

FACIAL PRODUCTS

☐ cleanser
☐ toner
☐ eye cleanser
☐ mask – non-setting
☐ moisturiser

CONTRA-INDICATIONS THAT RESTRICT TREATMENT
(Treatment may require adaption)

☐ cuts and abrasions
☐ recent scar tissue
☐ skin allergies
☐ bruising and swelling
☐ eczema
☐ psoriasis

SKIN CONDITION CHARACTERISTICS

☐ sensitive   ☐ mature
☐ dehydrated   ☐ milia
☐ broken capillaries   ☐ comedones
☐ pustules   ☐ papules
☐ open pores   ☐ hyper pigmentation
☐ hypo pigmentation   ☐ dermatitis
☐ keloids   ☐ papulosa nigra
☐ ingrowing hairs

EQUIPMENT AND MATERIALS

☐ magnifying light
☐ spatulas
☐ consumables
☐ protective covering

Therapist signature (for reference)

Client signature (confirmation of details)

TREATMENT ADVICE

 Basic facial treatment – *This treatment will take 35–45 minutes.*

TREATMENT PLAN

Record relevant details of your treatment and advice provided for future reference.

Ensure the client's records are up to date, accurate and fully completed following treatment. Non-compliance may invalidate insurance.

DURING

Find out:

- what products the client is currently using to cleanse and care for the skin of the face and neck
- how regularly the products are used
- satisfaction with their current skin-care routine
- Explain: how the products used should be applied and removed
- Note: any unwanted reaction (contra-action), if any occur

AFTER

Record:

- results of treatment
- what products have been used in the basic facial treatment
- the effectiveness of treatment
- any samples provided (review their success at the next appointment)
- Advice on: product application and removal in order to gain the best benefit from product use
- use of make-up following facial treatment
- the recommended time between each treatment
- the importance of a course of treatment to improve the skin condition

RETAIL OPORTUNITIES

Advise on:

- products that would be suitable for the client to use at home to care for their skin
- recommendations for further facial treatments
- further products or services that you have recommended that the client may or may not have received before.
- Note: any purchase made by the client

EVALUATION

Record:

- comments on the clients satisfaction with the treatment
- record how you will progress the treatment plan to maintain and advance the treatment results in the future

HEALTH AND SAFETY

Advise on :

- avoidance of activities or product application that may cause an unwanted skin reaction (contra-action)
- appropriate action to be taken in the event of an unwanted skin reaction

Equipment, materials and products used in a basic facial treatment

Product	Use	Health and safety practice
Bowls – various sizes	Holds client jewellery; skin-care preparations; cotton wool; warm water to remove face mask	Clean after use with a detergent, disinfect, rinse and dry. If using for water, keep on a stable surface to avoid spillage
Skin cleanser	Usually a combination of oil and water that is capable of dissolving grease and other substances from the skin's surface. Various cleansing preparations are available to the beauty therapist whose formulations are designed for different skin types	If a client has sensitive skin use a hypo-allergenic product. Use the correct cleansing product for the skin type to avoid skin irritation or sensitivity. Avoid excessive use of cleanser around the eye area to avoid cleanser entering the eye and causing eye irritation
Skin toner	Applied after the skin has been cleansed. Toning lotions remove all traces of cleanser and skin-care preparations from the skin's surface. They also create a skin-tightening effect, making the pores close. Various toning preparations are available, in formulations for the different skin types	If a client has sensitive skin use a hypo-allergenic product. Use the correct toning product for the skin type to avoid skin irritation or sensitivity. Replace lids immediately following use to avoid spillage. Gently blot the skin dry following application with a soft facial tissue to avoid stimulating the skin as the toner evaporates from the skin's surface
Eye make-up remover	Eye make-up remover cleanses the eyelids and lashes, gently dissolving make-up if worn. It also conditions the delicate skin. Formulated as a lotion or gel, it is designed to remove either water-based or oil-based products (or both)	If a client has sensitive skin use a hypo-allergenic product. Support the delicate eye tissue when cleansing the eye to avoid stretching the skin. Avoid excessive use of eye make-up remover as it may enter the eye causing irritation. Never apply pressure over the eyeball when cleansing the eye area
Moisturiser	The skin depends on water to keep it soft and supple. The natural moisture level is constantly being disturbed. The application of a cosmetic moisturiser helps to maintain the natural oil and moisture balance by locking moisture into the skin, offering protection and hydration. The basic formulation of a moisturiser is oil and water	If a client has sensitive skin use a hypo-allergenic product. Always use a spatula to remove moisturiser if in an open container to prevent contamination. Return lids immediately for hygiene and to prevent the quality of the product spoiling
Face mask	A cleansing preparation using a variety of different ingredients to absorb, cleanse, tighten (astringents), soften (emollients) and calm and soothe (desensitisers)	Clean the container following use. Ensure that product is taken from an open container using a clean spatula. Never place the mask brush on the client's skin and return to the product or contamination will occur
Mask brush	Used to apply face mask to the skin of the face and neck. Usually consists of a plastic handle with synthetic bristles	Clean in hot soapy water, allow to dry and store in the ultraviolet cabinet

Ellisons Salon System Salon System Ellisons Salon System Ellisons Ellisons

HEALTH AND SAFETY ✚

The autoclave
The autoclave – a sterilising unit similar to a pressure cooker – creates steam as the water inside it boils. A temperature of 121–134°C is reached and sterilises anything inside the autoclave. However, this process is only suitable for equipment that can withstand the heating process – check first.

Sterilisation and disinfection

It is important that hygienic practice is considered before and throughout the client treatment. This will help prevent cross-infection – the transfer of harmful bacteria/micro-organisms from one person to another.

All equipment should be sterilised or disinfected as appropriate prior to use on each client.

Hygiene checks

- Ensure that all tools and equipment are clean and sterile before use.
- Disinfect work surfaces regularly.
- Use disposable items whenever possible. Discard immediately after use in a covered, lined waste container.
- Follow hygienic practices.
- Maintain a high standard of personal hygiene.

Hygiene equipment

HEALTH AND SAFETY ✚

Eye make-up remover
If the client is wearing waterproof mascara, use an eye make-up remover designed to remove oil-based make-up. Non-oily make-up remover should be selected for a client wearing false eyelashes to prevent them being removed.

Equipment	Hygiene practice
Headband	A clean, freshly laundered headband should be provided for each client to prevent cross-infection. Several should be available to allow for drying time
Gowns and towels	All towels should be boil washed at 60° to destroy harmful micro-organisms following use. Clean towels and gowns should be provided for each client to prevent cross-infection
Treatment couch or beauty chair	The treatment couch should have an easy-to-clean surface. It should be cleaned daily with warm water and detergent. The surface of the treatment couch should be protected with clean towels and clean disposable paper roll for each client
Magnifying lamp	Check that the glass lens is cleaned after use
Spatula	Throw away after use
Workstation surface	Clean with a chemical disinfectant. Protect with clean disposable paper roll.

TIP ✓

Magnifying lamps
The magnifying lamp will provide the additional light required to magnify the surface of the skin during skin analysis and enable correct identification of skin type.

Preparation of the therapist

Ensure that the treatment area is warm and comfortable, ventilation is adequate and that lighting is adequate to induce relaxation, and to ensure that the treatment is performed competently. Check that the area is free from obstacles that could cause a fall.

Wash the hands, to remove surface dirt preventing cross-infection, this will also show the client you have good hygiene practice.

Follow proper hygiene and grooming procedures to ensure a professional image at all times.

Preparing the work area

Check the work area to make sure you have all the equipment, products and materials you require for the facial treatment. Use the checklist provided on page 97-8.

Prepare the treatment couch or beauty chair following salon policy.

Preparing the client – the consultation

The consultation should be carried out in the privacy of a treatment cubicle. It should take place when the client first meets you. The consultation enables the therapist to:

- assess whether the client is suitable for treatment or whether treatment is contra-indicated in some way
- ask the client specific questions about their current skin-care routine and general health. The client's answers will suggest to the therapist what is required, and what is achievable, from a skin-care programme.

During the consultation the therapist can also explain what is involved in the treatment, how long it takes and what aftercare and home-care is required.

Also during the consultation, the client will:

- discover what the beauty therapist can offer
- ask questions and receive honest professional advice concerning the most appropriate choice of skin-care product
- confirm and agree the treatment aim.

At the end of the consultation the client should fully understand what the proposed treatment involves:

1 Ask the client to remove jewellery from the treatment area, to prevent it becoming soiled by facial products. Place the jewellery in view of the client, usually in a tissue-lined bowl.
2 Offer the client a gown to wear. Position the client into a comfortable and relaxed position for treatment. The couch or beauty chair should offer adequate back support and be comfortable. Cover the client with a large bath towel. Drape a small hand towel across their shoulders.
3 Fasten a clean head-band around the client's hairline. Position the head-band so that it does not cover the skin of the face.
4 After preparing the client, wash your hands: this demonstrates to the client your concern to work hygienically.

TIP

Work area
The work area should be left ready for the next client on treatment completion. Waste products should be disposed of correctly following local council waste regulations. If you are free, assist other colleagues to tidy the area after treatment to maintain the work area in readiness for the next client.

Silhouette-Dermalift

Consultation prior to a facial treatment

HEALTH AND SAFETY

Posture
It is important that the client is positioned correctly on the couch. This will:

- ensure that the client is comfortable throughout the treatment and is supported properly
- prevent discomfort to the therapist, which may lead to muscle injury and long-term postural problems
- enable the treatment to be carried out properly.

TIP ✔

Communicating with your client

Communication includes talking with your client (verbal communication) and also what your body language is telling the client (non-verbal communication).

You might have given a client a great facial treatment but will you be asked to do it again if you are not bright, cheerful and helpful?

5 Check with the senior therapist that your facial treatment plan meets their satisfaction.

BASIC FACIAL TREATMENT PROCEDURE

Briefly, the stages in the basic facial treatment procedure are:

- skin cleansing
- toning
- application of a face mask
- moisturiser application.

Outcome 2: Carry out facial treatments

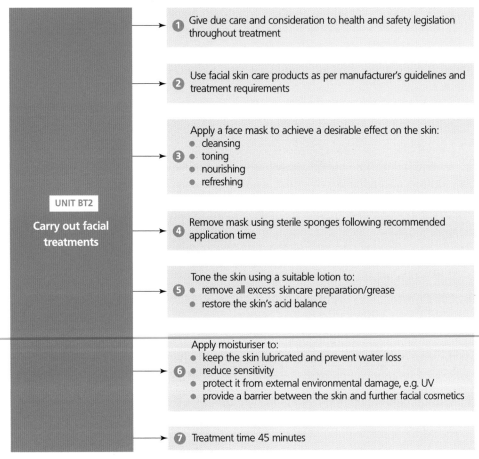

UNIT BT2

Carry out facial treatments

1 Give due care and consideration to health and safety legislation throughout treatment

2 Use facial skin care products as per manufacturer's guidelines and treatment requirements

3 Apply a face mask to achieve a desirable effect on the skin:
- cleansing
- toning
- nourishing
- refreshing

4 Remove mask using sterile sponges following recommended application time

5 Tone the skin using a suitable lotion to:
- remove all excess skincare preparation/grease
- restore the skin's acid balance

6 Apply moisturiser to:
- keep the skin lubricated and prevent water loss
- reduce sensitivity
- protect it from external environmental damage, e.g. UV
- provide a barrier between the skin and further facial cosmetics

7 Treatment time 45 minutes

Skin cleansing treatment

There are two parts in the cleansing routine:

1 The **superficial cleanse** uses lightweight cleansing preparations to emulsify surface make-up, dirt and grease.

2 The **deep cleanse** uses a heavier cleansing product – often a cream – which allows massage movements to be applied to the skin without the cleansing product evaporating.

Superficial cleansing

The face is cleansed in the following order:

1 the eye tissue and lashes
2 the lips
3 the neck, chin, cheeks and forehead.

Deep cleansing

The deep cleanse involves a series of massage movements using the hands and cleansing product. The skin becomes warm during the massage, which aids the absorption of the cleanser into the hair follicles and pores and increases the cleansing action.

TIP	✔

Choosing a cleansing product

Skin type	Cleansing product
Oily	Foaming cleanser / Cleansing lotion
Dry	Cleansing milk / Cleansing cream
Combination	Foaming cleanser / Cleansing lotion / Cleansing milk

Step by step: Superficial cleanse

HEALTH AND SAFETY	✚

Pressure
Reduce pressure when working over the neck.
Do not close the nostril openings when cleansing the nose.
Pressure must always be upwards and outwards to avoid stretching the delicate facial skin.

1 Wash your hands
2 Cleanse the eye area using a suitable eye make-up remover.
3 Each eye is cleansed separately supporting the delicate eye tissue with the non-working hand. Apply eye make-up remover (oily or non-oily) directly to clean, damp cotton wool. First, stroke down the length of the lashes, then cleanse the eye tissue in a sweeping circle, outwards across the upper eyelid, circling beneath the lower lashes towards the nose. Repeat, changing the cotton wool regularly until the eye area and cotton wool shows clean. Any make-up left along the lash line should be removed with a clean cotton bud.

4 Cleanse the lips, preferably with a cleansing milk or lotion. Apply a little product to damp cotton wool. Wipe the cleanser across the lips. Support the corner of the mouth with the non-working hand. Repeat, changing regularly the cotton wool until the lip area and cotton wool shows clean.
5 Select a cleansing product to suit your client's skin type: Whichever cleanser is chosen, it should have the following qualities:

- it should cleanse the skin effectively without causing irritation
- it should remove all traces of make-up and grease
- it should feel pleasant to use
- it should be easy to remove from the skin.

TIP ✓

Male client treatment
It is preferable to remove facial products with dampened sponges rather than cotton wool, which can drag and collect on coarse facial hair.

6 Apply the cleanser to the client's skin using your hands – sufficient to cover the face and neck – and massage gently over the surface of the skin. Using a series of light, circular movements with the fingertips, gently massage the product into the skin, beginning at the base of the neck and finishing at the forehead.

7 Remove the cleanser thoroughly, in an upwards and outwards direction, with clean damp cotton wool or facial sponges dampened with clean, warm water if preferred.

8 Repeat this process until all excess cleanser has been removed.

Step by step: Deep cleanse

1 Select and apply a suitable cleanser to the face and neck.

2 Stroke up both sides of the neck, using your fingertips. At the chin, draw the fingers outwards at the angle of the jaw and lightly stroke down to the neck to the starting position.

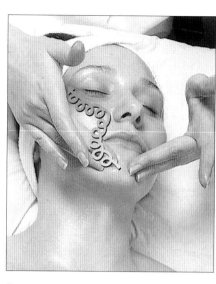

3 Apply small circular movements over the skin of the face and neck.

4 Draw the fingertips outwards to the angle of the jaw. Rest each index finger against the jaw bone. Place the middle finger beneath the jaw bone. Move the right hand towards the chin. When the index finger glides over the chin, return the fingers to the starting position beneath the jaw bone. Repeat with the left hand.

5 Apply circular movements, starting at the chin, working up towards the nose and finishing at the temples. Slide the fingers from the temples back to the chin, and repeat.

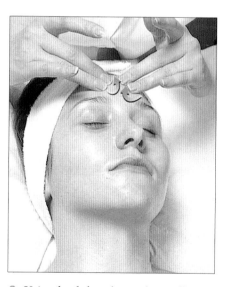

6 Position the ring finger of the right hand at the bridge of the nose. Perform a running movement, sliding the ring, middle and index fingers off the end of the nose. Repeat immediately with the left hand.

7 With the ring fingers, trace a circle around the eye. Begin at the inner corner of the upper brow bone; slide to the outer corners of the brow bone, around and under the eyes, and return to the starting position.

8 Using both hands, apply small circular movements across the forehead.

9 Open the index and middle fingers of each hand and perform a criss-cross stroking movement over the forehead.

10 Slide the index fingers upwards slightly, lifting the inner eyebrow. Lift the centre of the eyebrow with the middle finger. Finally, lift the outer corner of eyebrow with the ring finger. Slide the ring fingers around the outer corner and beneath the eye.

11 With the pads of each hand, apply slight pressure at the temples. This indicates to the client that the cleansing sequence is complete.

12 Remove the cleansing product from the skin, using damp cotton wool or facial sponges.

Skin toning

After the skin has been cleansed it is then toned with an appropriate lotion. Whichever toning lotion is chosen it should have the following qualities:

- it should produce a cooling effect on the skin when the water or alcohol evaporates from the skin's surface

- it should create a skin-tightening effect on the skin. This reduces the flow of sebum and sweat onto the skin's surface.

> **TIP**
>
> **Combination skin**
> If preferred, different toning lotions can be applied to treat the different skin types of a combination skin.

> **TIP**
>
> | Skin type | Toning lotion |
> | --- | --- |
> | Oily | **Astringents**, the strongest toning lotions with a high alcohol content to stimulate and promote skin healing |
> | Dry | Skin bracers and **skin fresheners**, the mildest toning lotions, contain little or no alcohol
They consist of mainly purified water and floral extracts for their toning properties |
> | Combination | **Skin tonics**, slightly stronger toning lotion than braces and freshens. Might contain a little of an astringent agent |

How to apply toner

1 Apply the selected toner to two pieces of clean damp cotton wool, which are wiped gently upwards and outwards over the surface of the skin.

2 The toner can be applied under pressure as a fine spray, using a vaporiser. This produces a fine mist of the toning lotion over the skin. Protect the eye tissue with damp cotton wool if using this technique.

3 After toner application, blot the skin dry with a soft facial tissue. Make a small tear in the centre of the tissue, for the client's nose. Place the tissue over the face and neck and mould it to the skin to absorb excess moisture.

The skin can be inspected at this stage using a cold light magnifier to illuminate the skin's surface to identify further facial characteristics.

Applying toner

Mask treatment

The face mask is applied when the skin has been thoroughly cleansed and toned. It is usually applied as the final facial treatment because of its cleansing, refining and soothing effects upon the skin. Select the appropriate mask ingredients to treat the skin type. There are two types of mask:

- **setting** masks: are applied in a thin layer over the skin's surface and are then allowed to dry

- **non-setting** masks: stay soft on application; they do not tighten like a setting mask.

You are required to competently apply a non-setting mask.

Blotting the skin

Non-setting mask

These are preprepared and have a softening and moisturising effect on the skin. Each mask contains various biological extracts or chemical substances to treat different skin conditions. Instructions will be provided with the mask, stating how the product is to be used professionally.

How to apply a non-setting mask

The method of mask preparation, application and removal are different for the various mask types. The guidelines below are for a non-setting, preprepared mask.

1 Select the non-setting mask suited to the client's skin type. Always read the manufacturer's instructions before applying.

TIP	✔

Maintaining the working area
It is important to work in a hygienic, organised manner, leaving the workstation neat and tidy and removing all waste materials both during and at the end of the treatment.

TIP ✓

Pre-prepared treatment mask
This type of mask is often available for retail sale to the client and will enable the client to continue to care for the skin at home

2 Discuss the treatment procedure with the client, in particular:

- what the mask will feel like on application
- what sensation the client is likely to experience
- how long the mask will be left on the skin.

Generally, the mask will be left in place for 10–20 minutes.

3 Using a clean mask brush, begin to apply the mask. The usual sequence of the mask application is neck, chin, cheeks, nose and forehead. Apply the mask evenly and quickly so that it has maximum effect on the whole face. Don't apply it too thickly; as well as making mask removal difficult it is wasteful as only the part that is in contact with skin has any effect. Keep the mask clear of the nostrils, the lips, the eyebrows and the hairline.

4 Apply dampened cotton wool pads over the eyes to relax the client.

5 Leave the mask for the recommended treatment time and according to the effect required.

6 Wash your hands.

7 When the mask is ready for removal, remove the eye pads.

8 Remove the mask using mask removal sponges, which should be damp – not wet – for client comfort and so that water does not run into the client's eyes, nose or hairline.

9 When the mask is thoroughly removed, apply the appropriate toning lotion. Blot the skin dry with a facial tissue.

Moisturiser application follows.

HEALTH AND SAFETY

Sensitive skin
It is important to discuss expected skin reactions and sensations with a client who has a sensitive skin so that client can tell you if there is a contra-action an unwanted skin reaction to the mask.

Mask application   Silhouette-Dermalift

Mask removal   Silhouette-Dermalift

TIP ✓

Selecting a moisturiser

Skin type	Moisturiser
Oily	Moisturising lotion
Dry	Moisturising cream
Combination	Moisturising lotion

A face mask treatment   Depilex/RVB

Skin moisturising

The basic formulation of a moisturiser is oil and water to make an oil-in-water emulsion. The water content helps to return lost moisture to the surface layers of the skin; the oil content prevents moisture loss from the surface of the skin. Often, a **humectant** ingredient is included, such as **glycerine**, which attracts moisture from the surrounding air and stops the moisturiser from drying out.

Moisturisers are available for wear during the day or night and are available in different formulations to suit different skin types. Select a moisturising day product to suit your client's skin type.

Whichever moisturiser is chosen, it should have the following qualities:

- it should soften the skin and relieve skin tightness and sensitivity
- it should plump out the skin's tissues with moisture, minimising the appearance of fine lines.

TIP ✓

Moisturiser formulations
Moisturising lotions contain 85–90 per cent water and 10–15 per cent oil
Moisturising creams contain 70–85 per cent water and 10–15 per cent oil
Hypoallergenic moisturisers are available for clients with sensitive skins. These are screened for all known common sensitising agents, such as lanolin and perfume.

TIP ✓

Moisturiser ingredients
Many moisturisers contain ingredients that improve the condition of the skin, such as vitamin E – an excellent skin conditioner – or ultraviolet filters to protect the skin from the premature ageing effects of sunlight.

Applying moisturiser

Spreading moisturiser evenly to the face and neck

How to apply moisturiser

Moisturiser is applied after the final application of toning lotion.

1 Place a small amount of moisturiser in the palms of the hands. If the product is in a jar, remove the moisturiser with a clean spatula.

2 Apply moisturiser on small dots to the neck, chin, cheeks, nose and forehead. Spread it quickly and evenly in a fine film over the face, using light upwards and outward stroking movements.

3 Blot excess moisturiser from the skin using a facial tissue.

COMPLETING FACIAL TREATMENTS

Make sure the client's records are up to date at the end of the treatment. This is important when you need to refer to them in the future. The record should then be stored securely.

The client should be given home-care advice so that the skin can be cared for at home. This will be different for each client, depending on individual needs.

Outcome 3: Complete treatments

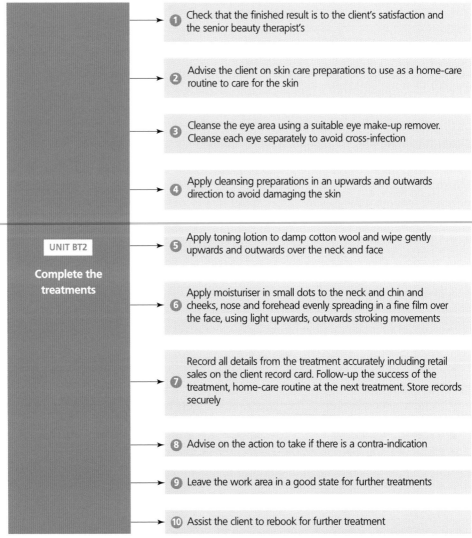

Complete the treatments

UNIT BT2

1 Check that the finished result is to the client's satisfaction and the senior beauty therapist's

2 Advise the client on skin care preparations to use as a home-care routine to care for the skin

3 Cleanse the eye area using a suitable eye make-up remover. Cleanse each eye separately to avoid cross-infection

4 Apply cleansing preparations in an upwards and outwards direction to avoid damaging the skin

5 Apply toning lotion to damp cotton wool and wipe gently upwards and outwards over the neck and face

6 Apply moisturiser in small dots to the neck and chin and cheeks, nose and forehead evenly spreading in a fine film over the face, using light upwards, outwards stroking movements

7 Record all details from the treatment accurately including retail sales on the client record card. Follow-up the success of the treatment, home-care routine at the next treatment. Store records securely

8 Advise on the action to take if there is a contra-indication

9 Leave the work area in a good state for further treatments

10 Assist the client to rebook for further treatment

Basic home-care and advice

- Discuss the use of make-up following treatment. Only lip and eye make-up should be worn directly after a facial treatment.

- Warn the client that a few blemishes might be experienced. These are caused by the cleansing action of the facial.

- If a client is given a sample of a treatment product, explain its correct use in terms of application and removal so that the client can gain maximum benefit from the product.

- Recommend the skin is cleansed and toned, twice a day, morning and night. Advise on the correct products to use.

- A moisturiser should be applied for day use and a separate moisturiser applied for night use. Each is formulated to achieve a different treatment effect. Advise on the correct products to use.

- The skin should be toned and moisturised following mask application.

- Advise the client on a treatment plan to improve the facial skin condition as necessary and what other professional treatments you could recommend within your responsibility.

- Advise the client that the correct treatment interval between facial treatments is usually 14–28 days.

Promoting products

Providing advice also gives you the opportunity to recommend retail products. This enhances the salon's retail sales and profit.

Contra-actions

Ask clients to contact the salon immediately and speak with the senior therapist if any unwanted reaction to the treatment occurs. Such *contra-actions* (e.g. an allergy, recognised by redness, swelling and inflammation) should be noted on the client's record for future reference.

Ensure the client's treatment card is completed accurately with all details of the treatment recorded. Store the record card securely in compliance with the Data Protection Act 1998.

ACTIVITY

Client satisfaction
It is important that the client enjoys their facial treatment as they will then most probably book to receive further treatments and long-term improvements in the skin will become noticeable.

However, the client may not have enjoyed the treatment because of how you performed it. With a colleague think of reasons why a client may not have been happy with the facial treatment.

Glossary

Acid mantle	acid film on the skin's surface created by a combination of sweat and sebum. The acid mantle is protective and discourages the growth of bacteria and fungi
Aftercare advice	recommended advice given to the client following treatment to continue the benefits of the treatment
Allergen	a substance that the skin is sensitive to and which causes an allergic reaction
Blood	nutritive liquid circulating through the blood vessels; transports essential nutrients to the cells and removes waste products; transports other important substances such as oxygen and hormones
Blood vessels	tubular structures in the body that carry blood
Cell	the smallest and simplest unit capable of life
Cleanser	a skin-care preparation that removes dead skin cells, excess sweat and sebum, make-up and dirt from the skin's surface to maintain a healthy skin complexion
Consultation	assessment of a client's needs using different assessment techniques, including questioning and natural observation
Contra-action	an unwanted reaction occurring during or after treatment application
Contra-indication	a problematic symptom that means that treatment might not proceed
Cross-infection	the transfer of contagious micro-organisms
Data Protection Act (1998)	legislation designed to protect client privacy and confidentiality
Deep cleanse	uses a heavier-than-usual cleansing product – often a cream – that allows massage movements to be applied to the skin without the cleansing product evaporating
Dermis	the inner portion of the skin, situated underneath the epidermis
Disinfection	The removal of micro-organisms by chemical or physical means
Epidermis	the outer layer of the skin
Facial	a treatment to improve the appearance, condition and functioning of the skin and underlying structures
Fibres	found in the dermis and give the skin its strength and elasticity. Yellow elastin gives the skin its elasticity, white collagen gives skin its strength
Fungus	microscopic plants that in humans, are parasites. Fungal diseases of the skin feed off the waste products of the skin. They are found on the skin's surface or they can attack deeper tissues.
Hair follicle	an appendage (structure) in the skin formed from epidermal tissue. Cells move up the hair follicle from the bottom (the hair bulb), changing in structure, to form the hair

Glossary

Hygiene	the recommended standard of cleanliness necessary in the salon to prevent cross-infection and secondary infection
Lymph	a clear, straw-coloured liquid circulating in the lymph vessels and lymphatics of the body, filtered out of the blood plasma.
Mask	a skin-cleansing treatment preparation applied to the skin. It might contain different ingredients to have a deep cleansing, toning, nourishing or refreshing effect. It can be applied to the hands, feet and/or face
Massage	manipulation of the soft tissues of the body, producing heat and stimulating the muscular, circulatory and nervous system
Melanin	a pigment in the skin that contributes to skin colour
Melanocytes	cells that produce the skin pigment melanin, which contributes to skin colour
Moisturiser	a skin-care preparation (formulation of oil and water) that helps maintain the skin's natural moisture by locking moisture into the skin, offering protection and hydration
Muscle	contractile tissue responsible for movement of the body
Muscle tone	the normal degree of tension in healthy muscle
Nerve	a collection of single neurons surrounded by a protective sheath through which impulses are transmitted between the brain or spinal cord and another part of the body
Papillae	projections near the surface of the dermis, which contain nerve endings and blood capillaries. These supply the upper epidermis with nutrition
Record cards	confidential cards recording personal details of each client registered at the salon
Sebaceous gland	a minute sac-like organ usually associated with the hair follicle. The cells of the gland decompose and produce the sebum. Found all over the body except the soles of the feet and the palms of the hands
Sebum	the skin's natural oil, which keeps the skin supple
Secondary infection	bacterial penetration into the skin causing infection
Skin allergy	if the skin is sensitive to a particular substance an allergic skin reaction will occur. This is recognised by irritation, swelling and inflammation
Skin analysis	assessment of the client's skin type and condition
Skin appendages	structures within the skin including sweat glands (that excrete sweat), hair follicles (that produce hair), sebaceous glands (that produce sebum) and nails – a horny substance that protects the ends of the fingers.
Skin tone	the strength and elasticity of the skin
Skin type	the different physiological functioning of each person's skin provides their skin type. Skin types include dry (lacking in oil), oily (excessive oil) and combination (a mixture of the other two skin types)

Glossary

Sterilisation	the total destruction of all micro-organisms
Subcutaneous tissue	a layer of fatty tissue situated below the epidermis and dermis
Superficial cleanse	uses light-weight cleansing preparations to emulsify surface make-up, dirt and grease
Sweat glands	small structures in the skin of the dermis and epidermis that excrete sweat. Their function is to regulate body temperature through the evaporation of sweat from the skin's surface
Toning lotion	a skin-care preparation to remove all traces of cleanser from the skin. It produces a cooling effect on the skin and has a skin tightening effect
Treatment plan	after the consultation, suitable treatment objectives are agreed to treat the client's condition and needs
Virus	virus particles invade healthy body cells and multiply within the cell. Eventually the virus kills the cell – the cell walls break down and the virus particles are freed to attack further cells

Assessment of knowledge and understanding

Unit BT2: Assist with facial treatments

You have now learnt about the different products and treatments that you can apply to the skin of the face and neck, this will enable you to assist with facial treatments. To test your level of knowledge and understanding, answer the following short questions. These will prepare you for your summative (final) assessment.

Anatomy and physiology

1 Name three functions of the skin.

2 How many layers of the epidermis are there?

3 What is the dermis?

4 Where is the dermis situated?

5 Label the features of the cross-section of the skin shown below:

Prepare for facial treatments:

1 What details should be recorded on the client's record card?

2 At the consultation you notice a client has a crusty blemish by her lip. What action do you take?

3 How do you identify a client's skin type and treatment requirements?

4 How should all client records be stored to comply with the Data Protection Act (1998)?

5 Name four facial conditions that would contra-indicate treatment.

6 How should you prepare yourself for the treatment? (Remember to consider health and safety requirements.)

7 How can you ensure client comfort when preparing the facial treatment area?

Carry out facial treatments

1 How long would you allow for a complete basic facial treatment?

Assessment of knowledge and understanding

2 Design a facial treatment, lasting 45 minutes, for a client with a dry skin type. Describe:

a the aim of the facial treatment
b the facial skin products you are going to use
c the aftercare advice to be given to maintain the skin condition.

Consider what products the client should be recommended to use at home and how to use them.

3 Why is it important to keep accurate records of the client's treatment?

4 What is the purpose of the following skin-care products?

a cleanser
b toning lotion
c moisturiser
d face mask.

Complete the treatments

1 What skin-care products would you recommend that a client use as part of her homecare routine?

2 How would you explain to the client the correct application and – where relevant – removal of the following products for home use?

a cleansing milk
b toning lotion
c non-setting face mask.

3 How often would you recommend a basic facial treatment?

4 How should the treatment area be left following each treatment, and why?

chapter 5

BT3 Assist with nail treatments on the hands

Learning objectives

This chapter covers the skills and knowledge you need to assist with and provide basic nail treatments on the hands. It describes the competencies to enable you to:

- prepare for nail treatments

- carry out nail treatments

- complete the treatments.

When performing nail treatments, it is important at all times to consider all health and safety requirements using the knowledge you gained from Unit G1: Ensure your own actions reduce risks to health and safety (see Chapter 1).

Creative Nails

Great nails are part of good grooming

PRACTICAL SKILLS AND KNOWLEDGE

The table shown here will help you to check your progress in gaining the necessary practical skills and knowledge for Unit BT3: Assist with nail treatments on the hands.

Tick (✓), when you feel you have gained your practical skills and knowledge in the following areas:

Practical skills and knowledge checklist	✓
1 The treatment aim of a basic nail treatment	
2 Contra-indications which prevent a nail treatment	
3 Equipment and products that are needed	
4 How to prepare the treatment area	
5 How to prepare yourself before the nail treatment	
6 Client consultation	
7 How to prepare the client	
8 How to carry out the basic nail treatment	
9 After-care and advice to be given to the client following treatment	
10 Contra-actions to look for during or following the nail treatment	

When you have ticked all the areas you can, ask your assessor to assess you on Unit BT3: Assist with nail treatments on the hands. After practical assessment, your assessor might decide that you still need to practise further to improve your skills. If so, your assessor will tell you how and where you need to improve to gain competence.

BASIC NAIL TREATMENTS

The basic nail treatment aims to improve the appearance of the:

- hands
- cuticles
- nails.

The hands

Healthy hands have soft, smooth skin. Wear and tear, or neglect, can make the skin dry, chapped, irritated, rough and even broken.

When carrying out basic nail treatment, your aim is to maintain or return the skin to a healthy, soft and smooth condition. This might take more than one treatment and you will need to advise the client on how to care for the hands at home; this is called aftercare and advice.

The cuticles

The cuticle is the part of the skin found around the base of the nail. When in a good condition, the cuticle is soft and loose. However, it easily becomes dry, tight, split and overgrown at the base of the nail.

When carrying out the basic nail treatment, your aim is to soften and moisturise the cuticles. After-care advice must always be given so that clients know how to care for the cuticles themselves.

The nails

The nails should be smooth, supple and have a healthy pink appearance. The edge that is filed (the free edge) should be even in shape. The nails can lose their healthy pink colour and become ridged, pitted, brittle and bruised, and the free edge is easily split and broken.

When carrying out the basic nail treatment, your aim is to maintain or improve the healthy pink colour of the nail, improve the smoothness and suppleness of the nail and file the free edge to a suitable even, shape and length.

After-care advice must always be given so that clients know how to care for the nails themselves.

You need to know about the different parts of the nail if you are to be able to improve its appearance and care properly for the nail.

ANATOMY AND PHYSIOLOGY

Nail parts and functions

The basic nail unit

Nails grow from the ends of the fingers and toes and their main purpose is to form a hard protective shield. When healthy the nails appear a pink colour with a smooth even surface.

ACTIVITY

Skin conditions on the hand
Why can the skin on the hands become dry, chapped, irritated, rough or broken?
You need to ask the client questions to find out a cause for the skin's appearance, and then you can give helpful advice.
Discuss with your salon colleagues possible causes for the poor skin condition.

Healthy hands, cuticles and nails
Jessica Nails

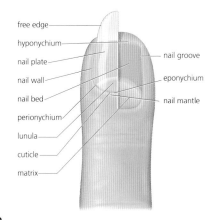

free edge
hyponychium
nail plate
nail wall
nail bed
perionychium
lunula
cuticle
matrix
nail groove
eponychium
nail mantle

Parts of the nail

HEALTH AND SAFETY ✚

Damage to the matrix
If damage occurs to the matrix it can affect the health and appearance of the nail. For example, if the matrix is injured due to accidental damage such as a blow to the nail, permanent furrows or ridges might appear on the nail plate. The appearance of these ridges can be reduced by the application of a ridge-filling base coat.
If injury is serious the nail plate can be lost, and might never grow back.

A nail showing ridges in the nail plate due to damage to the matrix   Dr A.L. Wright

Matrix

The matrix is found at the bottom of the nails and is the growing area of the nail. It is made up of **cells** – tiny particles that make up all living things. The cells in this area divide continuously to produce the nail plate.

The matrix: growing area of the nail

The nail plate

The nail plate is the correct name for the part of the nail that covers the **nail bed**, the portion of skin on which the nail plate rests. The cells here are clear and have hardened. These hard cells serve to protect the nail bed below and, because they are clear, allow you to see if the living nail bed is a healthy pink colour. The function of the nail plate is to protect the nail bed.

The nail grows forward slowly over the nail bed, at a rate of 0.5 mm to 1.2 mm per week. It takes between four and six months for a nail plate to grow fully from cuticle to free edge.

Nail plate: covers and protects the nail bed

The nail bed

The nail bed is the part of the skin covered by the nail plate. The nail plate and nail bed separate at the free-edge end of the finger. The nail bed is made up of living cells and contains many **blood vessels**, which carry blood which provides the nourishment necessary for healthy growth and repair; the nail bed also contains **nerves** that enable you to sense pain, heat, etc. The functions of the nail bed are to supply nourishment and protection.

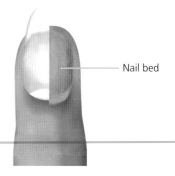

The nail bed: provides nourishment and protection

Cuticle

The cuticle is the overlapping skin at the bottom of the nail plate that grows forward onto the nail plate. When overgrown, it can grow high up onto the nail plate and will often split, which can then become infected. It is important to keep the cuticles soft and loose. The function of the cuticle is to protect the nail bed from infection.

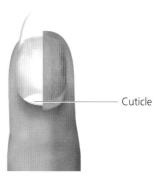

The cuticle: protects the nail bed from infection

Free edge

The free edge is the part of the nail that grows beyond the fingertip. It is usually white, as it does not have the pink nail bed below it. It is the part of the nail that is filed and shaped. The function of the free edge is to protect the fingertip.

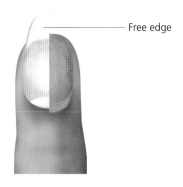

Free edge

The free edge: protects the finger tip

Nail shapes

Each client's hand size, finger length and nail shape is unique to them. It is important that the nail shape and length selected suits the client's hands and fingers. The nail plate free edge can be shaped to improve the appearance of the hands and fingers. Nail shapes include:

- Oval: the sides of the free edge are curved. This is an ideal shape for short, stubby fingers as it makes the fingers appear slimmer and longer.
- Square: the free edge is filed straight across. This nail shape will improve the appearance of thin, long fingers, making the fingers appear shorter and fuller.
- Squoval: a combination of oval and square nail shape. The nail is filed to a square finish at the free edge and is then gently curved at the corners.
- Round nails: the free edge is rounded and is an ideal shape for short nails. This style is popular with male clients.
- Pointed: avoid pointed nails shapes as this shape weakens the nail at the sides and it breaks easily.
- Fan: the nail becomes broader as it grows towards the free edge, appearing as a fan shape. The wider sides of the nail at the free edge should be shaped to achieve an oval shape.

TIP ✓

Nail growth
Nails grow faster in summer than in winter; faster in young people than in older people; faster on the hand that is most often used, i.e. if you are right handed this will be the one that the nails grows quickest. Illness and medication can affect nail growth, speeding it up or slowing it down.

Oval   Square   Squoval   Round   Pointed   Fan

TIP ✓

Pain
There are no blood vessels or nerves in the nail plate and free edge: this is why it can be cut without pain or bleeding.

NAIL TREATMENT

When a client makes an appointment for a basic nail treatment, the receptionist should ask a few basic questions:

- What is the client's name and telephone number? This will help you to get the client record card ready before they arrive for treatment. The telephone number is important in case you need to cancel the treatment for any reason, e.g. the beauty therapist is ill.

- Which therapist does the client want to see? If a particular therapist is needed you will have to check on availability.
- When does the client want the treatment, e.g. day/date and time? If any of these are not available, suggest another time or day as near to this as possible.
- Has the client had the treatment before? This allows the client to ask you questions about the treatment. You may explain what a basic nail treatment includes.

A basic nail treatment includes:

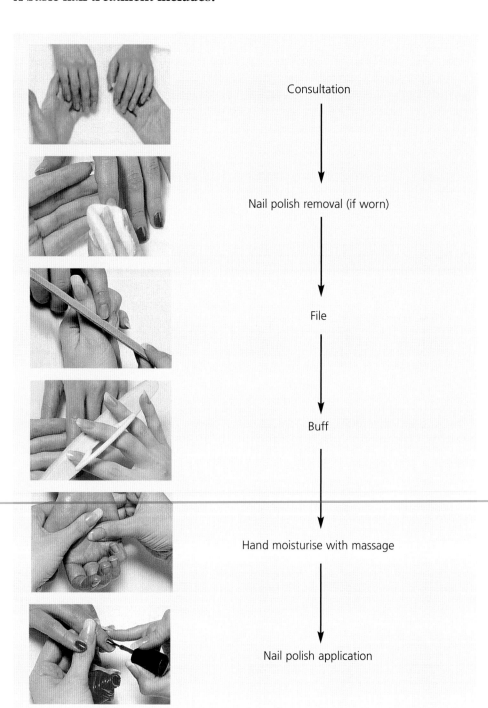

Consultation

↓

Nail polish removal (if worn)

↓

File

↓

Buff

↓

Hand moisturise with massage

↓

Nail polish application

ACTIVITY

Treatment times
What is the time allowed for a basic nail treatment?
Why is it important to complete the treatment in this time?
Think of three reasons for both.

- Does the client require any other services in addition to the basic nail treatment? Always look at opportunities to increase treatment bookings, the salon needs to keep busy!

Remember, when making an appointment it is important to allow enough time to complete the treatment properly. It is also important for the therapist to be able to complete the treatment in a commercially acceptable time.

TIP ✓

Timing
Allow 30 minutes for a basic nail treatment.

The Data Protection Act (1998)

The client's personal details are recorded on their record card.

These details are confidential, or private. All information relating to a client should be stored securely. Only those staff with permission to access it can do so. Therefore, as soon as all treatment details have been recorded on the record card, the client's details should be stored securely.

It is important that all details are accurate and up to date.

Before treatment

Before treatment is carried out you will need to prepare the work area, yourself and the client for the treatment.

Contra-indications to treatment

Certain nail, hand and skin conditions prevent or restrict you from performing the basic nail treatment. These are known as **contra-indications**. If, when looking at a client's hands and nails before the treatment you think you recognise any of the following conditions, you must not perform basic nail treatment. You will need to refer the client tactfully to the relevant person in the salon for confirmation that the treatment can go ahead (or not).

HEALTH AND SAFETY

Contra-indications
Remember, you might be wrong when you think you have a client with a contra-indication. Always check with the senior therapist – the client may be able to have the treatment after all.
Never diagnose, and try to avoid causing the client embarrassment. The senior therapist may recommend that the client seeks medical advice before manicure treatment goes ahead.

Contra-indications that prevent treatment

Many of the skin and nail conditions in the table below are contagious – they can be passed to other clients and clients with these conditions should never be treated.

Name of contra-indication	Cause	Appearance
Impetigo	A **contagious** bacterial infection caused by minute, single-celled organisms and which results in **skin** inflammation	The skin appears red and is itchy. Small blisters appear, which burst and then form crusts
Warts **Common wart**: found on the hand **Plane wart**: found on the fingers or either surface of the hands	Contagious **viral** infection that results in abnormal skin growth A contagious **fungal** infection of the skin. Fungal diseases of the skin feed off the waste products of the skin	Small skin growths, varying in size, shape, texture and colour. Usually raised with a rough surface. Found on the fingers, either surface of the hand
Scabies or **itch mites**	A contagious **infestation** caused by an **animal parasite** that burrows beneath the skin and enters the hair follicles	Small lumps and wavy greyish lines appear on the skin. This is where dirt has entered where the parasite burrows under the skin. Found in warm, loose areas of skin such as in between the fingers and the creases of the elbows
Tinea corporis or **body ringworm**	A contagious **fungal** infection of the skin, caused by microscopic plants. Fungal diseases of the skin feed off the waste products of the skin and are parasitic	Small, scaly red patches spread outwards and then heal from the centre, leaving a ring. Found on the limbs
Tinea unguium or **nail ringworm**	A contagious **fungal** infection of the nail plate	The nail plate is yellowish grey. Eventually the nail plate becomes brittle and separates from the nail bed

Dr M H Beck

Name of contra-indication	Cause	Appearance
Broken bones 	Injury – should be treated medically	The breakage might not be obvious. If the client is new, check that there have been no broken bones at the consultation. The broken bone must not be handled. Therefore, if one finger is broken you must avoid this finger. Always check first with the relevant person in the workplace
Severe nail separation-onycholysis 	Lifting of the nail plate from the nail bed, may be caused by trauma or infection to the nail or surrounding area	Where separation has occurred this appears as a greyish white area on the nail as the pink colour of the nail bed does not show.
Paronychia 	Infectious bacterial infection	Swelling, redness, and pus appears in the cuticle area of the skin around the nail
Cuts or abrasions on the hands	Injury to the skin	Broken skin
Severe psoriasis of the nail	An inflammatory condition where there is increased cell production and thickening of the nail	A pitting effect can occur on the surface of the nail plate like the surface of an orange. Nail separation may also occur
Severe eczema of the nail	Inflammation of the skin, which may cause differing changes to the nail	Ridges, pitting, nail separation and even nail loss may occur

Wellcome Photo Library

Wellcome Photo Library

HEALTH AND SAFETY ✚

Broken skin

If a client has a minor, small scratch of the skin in the treatment area, treatment can usually go ahead by avoiding contact with the area, with permission of the senior therapist. If the client has a cut, redness and swelling the treatment should not go ahead. If unsure, seek guidance from the senior therapist first.

Nail and skin conditions that might restrict treatment

The nail and skin conditions below are non-contagious and cannot be passed to other clients. You can therefore treat a client with one of these conditions, although you might need to adapt your treatment application.

Name of contra-indication	Cause	Appearance	Treatment
Bruised nail	Damage to the nail (e.g. by trapping in a door)	Part or all of the nail plate appears blue or black	Avoid the nail that is bruised when carrying out the nail treatment
Onychopagy	Excessive nail biting	Very little nail plate. The skin appears red and swollen due to biting of the skin around the nails	Regular weekly nail treatments to encourage nail growth and treat any dry skin and cuticle. The client could try applying bitter-tasting nail preparations at home to prevent nail biting
Pterygium	Neglect	Overgrown cuticles, tightly attached to the nail plate. When left untreated they often split and crack	Advise the client to have a manicure where the excess cuticle can be removed using specialised tools called *nippers* or *clippers*. The client should be advised to apply a rich cuticle treatment cream daily
Ridges in the nail plate	Illness, damage or old age	Ridges in the nail plate running across or down the length of the nail plate, from the cuticle to the free edge. This can affect one or all nails	Buffing treatment to help to improve the appearance of the nail by smoothing out the ridges. A ridge-filling base coat can also be applied before nail polish application
Hangnail	Dry skin or cuticle that cracks. Biting the skin around the nail	The skin around the nail plate cracks and a small piece of skin appears between the nail plate and side of the nail (nail wall). Sometimes the area becomes red and swollen	Specialised manicure treatment to soften the skin and cuticles. Removal of the excess skin using cuticle nippers. Advise the client to apply hand cream and cuticle cream to prevent dryness
Leuconychia	Damage to the nail plate due to pressure or hitting with a hard object	White spots appear on the nail plate, which grow out with the nail	Advise the client to take general care of the nails. Recommend the application of a coloured nail polish to disguise the white spots

Dr A.L. Wright

Dr A.L. Wright

Dr A.L. Wright

Dr A.L. Wright

Judith Ford

Dr A.L. Wright

Name of contra-indication	Cause	Appearance	Treatment
Onychorrhexis	Poor diet Harsh detergents Incorrect choice/use of manicure products	Split, flaking nails	Ensure a balanced diet. Regular use of a hand cream. Protect the nails from detergents, which dry the nails, always wear rubber gloves. Nail treatment base polishes can have specific effects to improve the nail. Incorrect use/choice can dry the nails causing the nails to split and flake
Non-severe skin eczema	Inflammation of the skin caused by contact with a skin irritant	The skin becomes red, swells and blisters can appear. The blisters burst, which then causes scabs to form on the skin. Often affects the inner creases of the elbows	Ensure you find out what irritants make the eczema worse and avoid contact with such products, e.g. perfumed products. The skin can benefit from massage lotion that contains soothing ingredients such as lavender. Do not treat if the skin is broken
Non-severe skin psoriasis	Cause unknown but becomes worse when the person is stressed Often hereditary	Itchy, red, flaky patches of skin, which can become infected if the skin becomes broken. Found on the elbows	The skin can benefit from massage lotion that contains soothing ingredients such as lavender. Do not treat if the skin is broken
Non-severe nail psoriasis	Psoriasis of the nail can cause further nail disorders to occur. Cause unknown but becomes worse when the person is stressed. Often hereditary	Pitting and discolouration of the nail plate with possible increased nail curvature and nail thickening.	Take care when treating the nails. It is advisable to keep the nails short
Non-severe nail eczema	Inflammation of the skin, causing changes to the nail	Ridges and pitting of the nails	Take care when treating the nails. It is advisable to keep the nails short

Photo credits: Dr A.L. Wright, Dr M.H. Beck, Dr M.H. Beck

HEALTH AND SAFETY

Skin disorders

If a client has nail or skin disorders that have only recently appeared, ask that client to consult a GP on the suitability of nail treatment. This would be relevant for all contra-indications plus those conditions that restrict treatment, mainly eczema and psoriasis.

Before treating any client, if you are at all unsure check with the relevant person in the workplace.

Outcome 1: Prepare for nail treatments

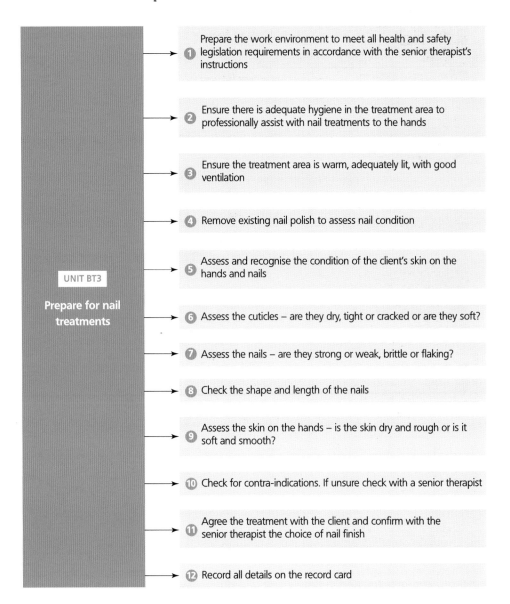

UNIT BT3

Prepare for nail treatments

1. Prepare the work environment to meet all health and safety legislation requirements in accordance with the senior therapist's instructions

2. Ensure there is adequate hygiene in the treatment area to professionally assist with nail treatments to the hands

3. Ensure the treatment area is warm, adequately lit, with good ventilation

4. Remove existing nail polish to assess nail condition

5. Assess and recognise the condition of the client's skin on the hands and nails

6. Assess the cuticles – are they dry, tight or cracked or are they soft?

7. Assess the nails – are they strong or weak, brittle or flaking?

8. Check the shape and length of the nails

9. Assess the skin on the hands – is the skin dry and rough or is it soft and smooth?

10. Check for contra-indications. If unsure check with a senior therapist

11. Agree the treatment with the client and confirm with the senior therapist the choice of nail finish

12. Record all details on the record card

Equipment and materials

Before carrying out the basic manicure, check that you have all the necessary equipment and materials to hand.

Refer to the equipment and materials checklist to make sure that you have all that is required to perform a basic nail treatment. Tick in the box next to each item on the checklist to help you as you prepare the work area.

EQUIPMENT, MATERIALS AND PRODUCTS CHECKLIST

Manicure table or trolley – on which to place everything ☐

Small bowls lined with tissues (2) – one for the client's jewellery
and one for clean cotton wool ☐

Towels (2) – freshly laundered for each client ☐

Finger bowl to place the fingers in warm water to soften the cuticles ☐

Emery board to shape the free edge ☐

Orange sticks to remove products hygienically and to gently loosen
the cuticle and clean under the free edge ☐

Nail polish remover to remove previous polish worn by the client
and to remove any polish that is accidentally placed on the
surrounding cuticle or skin ☐

Coloured nail polish – a range of colours suited to the client's nails and choice ☐

Base coat to prevent staining of the nail plate and improve the nail appearance ☐

Specialist nail treatment polishes, i.e. nail strengthener ☐

Top coat to seal, provide shine and protect the nail polish ☐

Nail scissors to reduce the length of the nail before filing ☐

Buffers to remove surface cells on the nail plate achieving a smoother
nail plate and increasing blood circulation to nourish the nail bed ☐

Buffing paste – a gritty paste used to remove surface cells and give a
shine to the nail plate ☐

Client's record card to record all client's personal details and record
details of the treatment before and following the treatment ☐

Cotton wool to remove old nail enamel and excess oils from the nails
before nail polish application ☐

Tissues to place over the sanitised nail equipment and line the bowls
as necessary ☐

Lined waste bin to collect waste materials during and following treatment ☐

Disinfecting solution to keep the small tools hygienic once sterilised ☐

Skin cleanser to cleanse the client's skin before you begin the treatment ☐

Client Record Card, and treatment plan details for you to complete before, during and following treatment

BEAUTY WORKS

Date	Therapist name	
Client name		Date of birth
Address		Postcode
Evening phone number	Day phone number	
Name of doctor	Doctor's address and phone number	
Related medical history (conditions that may restrict or prohibit treatment application)		
Are you taking any medication?		

CONTRA-INDICATIONS REQUIRING MEDICAL REFERRAL
(Preventing **manicure treatment** application)

- ☐ bacterial infection (e.g. paronychia)
- ☐ viral infection (e.g. plane warts)
- ☐ fungal infection (e.g. tinea ungium)
- ☐ severe nail separation
- ☐ severe eczema and psoriasis
- ☐ severe bruising
- ☐ broken bones

EQUIPMENT AND MATERIALS

- ☐ nail and skin treatment tools
- ☐ abrasives (e.g. buffing cream)
- ☐ nail and skin products
- ☐ nail conditioners (e.g. cuticle cream/oil)
- ☐ skin conditioners (e.g. hand cream)
- ☐ consumables

CONTRA-INDICATIONS THAT RESTRICT TREATMENT
(Treatment may require adaption)

- ☐ minor nail separation
- ☐ mild psoriasis/eczema
- ☐ recent scar tissue
- ☐ severely bitten nails
- ☐ severely damaged nails
- ☐ minor cuts and abrasions
- ☐ minor bruising and swelling

TREATMENT AIM

- ☐ improvement of skin condition

    products used _____

- ☐ improvement of nail condition

    products used _____

NAIL FINISH

- ☐ buffing
- ☐ clear polish
- ☐ nail strengthener

NAIL, CUTICLE AND SKIN CONDITION

nails	cuticle	skin
☐ normal	☐ dry	☐ dry
☐ brittle	☐ split	☐ hard
☐ dry	☐ overgrown	
☐ weak		
☐ ridged		

MASSAGE MEDIUMS

- ☐ creams
- ☐ oils

Therapist signature (for reference)

Client signature (confirmation of details)

BEAUTY WORKS *(continued)*

TREATMENT ADVICE

 Basic hand/nail treatment – *allow 30 minutes.*

TREATMENT PLAN

Record relevant details of your treatment and advice provided for future reference.

Ensure the client's records are up to date, accurate and fully completed following treatment. Non-compliance may invalidate insurance.

DURING

Discuss:

- details that may influence the client's nail condition such as occupation
- products the client is currently using to care for the skin of the hands and nails and how often they are used
- the client's satisfaction with these products

Explain:

- relevant manicure procedures (e.g. how to file the nails correctly)

Note:

- any unwanted reaction (contra-action), if any occur

AFTER

Record:

- results of treatment
- what products have been used in the basic hand/nail treatment
- the effectiveness of treatment (where you happy with the result?)
- any samples provided (ask the client what they thought of them at the next appointment)

Advise on:

- product application in order to gain the best benefit from product use
- use of specialised products following manicure treatment for home care use, such as nail strengthener
- general hand/nail care

Discuss:

- the recommended time between each treatment
- the importance of a course of treatment to improve nail/skin conditions

RETAIL OPPORTUNITIES

Advise on:

- products that would be suitable for the client to use at home to care for the skin of the hands and nails
- recommendations for further treatments
- further products or services that you have recommended that the client may or may not have received before

Note:

- any purchase made by the client

EVALUATION

Record:

- comments on the client's satisfaction with the treatment
- if poor results are achieved, the reasons why

Note:

- if necessary, how you may alter the treatment plan to achieve the required treatment results in the future

HEALTH AND SAFETY

- Advise on the correct action to be take in the event of an unwanted skin or nail reaction (contra-action)

Equipment materials and products used in a basic nail treatment

Read and follow manufacturers' instructions before using all manicure products. Have a Material Data Safety Sheet (MSDS) available for all products that you use in your treatment. Each beauty supplier is legally required to provide guidelines on how materials should be used and stored in compliance with the legislation the Control of Substances Hazardous to Health (COSHH) Regulations 2002.

Product	Use	Health and safety practice
Sterilising fluid Ellisons	Sterilising fluid that prevents the multiplication of micro-organisms but does not kill all micro-organisms. Objects must be kept sanitary once sterilised	Could cause a slip hazard if spilt. Might cause skin irritation and is toxic if swallowed. Chemical sterilising sprays are also used to sterilise the surface of manicure tools. These should be used following manufacturer's instructions and in a well-ventilated area, avoiding contact with flame and excessive heat
Finger bowl	Fill with warm water and add a pleasant smelling nail soak to cleanse and soften the cuticles	Clean after use with a detergent, disinfect, rinse and dry. When in use keep on a stable surface to avoid spillage
Emery board Ellisons	A nail file used to shape the nails. It usually has two sides; one side is coarser than the other	Use a new emery board for each client to avoid cross-infection. Use the coarser side to reduce length of the nail. Never use a sawing action when filing as you can cause the free edge to split
Orange sticks Ellisons	Disposable wooden tools, usually with a hoof-shaped end for use around the cuticle and a pointed end for cleaning under the free edge. They can also be used to remove product from containers	Never reuse the orange sticks: throw away after the treatment to avoid cross-infection. Always tip with clean cotton wool if used to clean under the free edge. Used incorrectly on the nail they could pierce the skin
Nail scissors Ellisons	Used to shorten long nails before filing	Support the nails at the side of the nail plate with the other hand to avoid client discomfort and ensure that all pieces of nail can be collected and thrown away. Sterilise nail scissors between each client to avoid cross-infection
Buffers	Use to improve the surface appearance of the nail, stimulate blood circulation to the nail bed and impart shine to the nail plate. The buffer might have a plastic handle and a replaceable pad covered with soft leather. This buffer can be used with or without buffing paste. Also available are four-sided nail buffers, similar to a thick emery board with a choice of surfaces from slightly coarse to very smooth, these are used without buffing paste	Ensure that the soft leather cover is replaced for each client to avoid cross-infection. This means you will need more than one cover. Do not over-use the coarse buffer or the nail will become thin and weakened

Product	Use	Health and safety practice
Skin cleanser IBD	A chemical that removes a number of harmful micro-organisms from the client's skin that could cause infection. This cleansing process is called sanitisation and an antiseptic product is often used	Antiseptics can be used safely on the skin but some clients might have an intolerance to them, leading to an allergic reaction. Always check at consultation if the client has any known skin allergies
Nail polish remover Millennium Nails	A product that will dissolve and remove nail polish and grease from the nail plate. The ingredient that causes this is called *acetone*.	Nail polish remover can be drying to the nail: choose one that contains oils. Store away from heat as it is highly flammable
Nail polish: coloured basecoat topcoat Salon Systems	Can be applied to improve the natural appearance of the nail, or add colour and protection	Always secure the lid tightly after use to avoid the product spoiling and accidental spillage. Ensure that the client is not allergic; some clients have allergies to the ingredient *formaldehyde* in nail polish
Nail strengthener Salon Systems	A nail polish product that strengthens a nail plate that has a tendency to split in layers, usually a dry, brittle nail	Check if the client has known allergies, some clients have allergies to the ingredient *formaldehyde*, which is sometimes found in nail strengthener
Buffing paste Ellisons	A coarse cream containing ingredients such as pumice or talc to remove the surface cells of the nail plates, giving shine	Avoid over-use of the buffing paste to avoid thinning and weakening of the nail plate
Hand cream/oil Salon Systems	A mixture of waxes and oils with perfumes and preservatives to maintain its quality. Hand creams/oils soften the skin of the hands and cuticles and assist the application of massage movements	Some hand massage products contain lanolin, a skin moisturising agent that can cause an allergic skin reaction. Always check if the client has any known allergies before treatment, and know your product ingredients

HEALTH AND SAFETY

The autoclave
A sterilising unit similar to a pressure cooker – creates steam as the water inside it boils. A temperature of 121–134°C is reached, which is sufficient to sterilise the items inside the autoclave. This process is only suitable for equipment that can withstand the heating process – always check first.
When possible, use equipment that can be thrown away after use (disposable), e.g. emery boards and orange sticks.

HEALTH AND SAFETY

Nail Services: A Code of Practice
Habia has produced a Code of Practice in nail services that provides guidance on the correct hygiene procedures and working practices to prevent cross-infection and ensure a professional service and profile is achieved.
The code of practice is available to download from the Habia website: www.habia.org.

Sterilisation and disinfection

It is important that hygienic practice is considered before and throughout the client treatment. This will help prevent cross-infection – the transfer of harmful bacteria/micro-organisms from one person to another.

All equipment should be sterilised or disinfected as appropriate prior to use on each client.

Hygiene checks

- Ensure that all tools and equipment are clean and sterile before use.
- Disinfect work surfaces regularly.
- Use disposable items whenever possible. Discard immediately after use in a covered, lined waste container.
- Follow hygienic practices.
- Maintain a high standard of personal hygiene.

Hygiene equipment

Equipment	Hygiene practice
Scissors	Clean with a disinfectant and autoclave Store in ultraviolet cabinet before use
Buffer	Wipe handle with surgical spirit Wash buffing cloth in hot soapy water 60°C Place in ultraviolet cabinet when dry
Emery board	Throw away after use
Orange stick	Throw away after use
Manicure bowl	Clean with a chemical disinfectant that will not damage the plastic surface
Spatula	Throw away after use
Workstation surface	Clean with a chemical disinfectant. Protect surfaces with clean disposable paper roll

Ellisons

Ellisons

Ellisons

Ellisons

Millennium Nails

Preparation of the therapist

Make sure the treatment area is warm and comfortable, ventilation is adequate and that lighting is adequate to prevent eye strain and to enable the treatment to be performed competently. Check that the area is free from obstacles that could cause a fall.

Wash the hands to remove surface dirt, preventing cross-infection, this will also show the client you have good hygiene practice.

Follow proper hygiene and grooming procedures to ensure a professional image at all times.

Preparing the work area

Check the work area to ensure that you have all the equipment, products and materials you require for the nail treatment. Use the checklist provided on page 131.

Place a clean towel over the work surface, then fold another towel into a pad and place it in the middle of the work surface. This will help support the client's forearm during treatment. Place a third towel over the pad.

The therapist will need a small towel to dry the client's hands during the treatment.

A tissue or disposable manicure mat should then be placed on top of the towels, to collect filings. This is disposed of later to avoid skin irritation from the filings.

How to prepare the client

1 Help the client into a comfortable and relaxed position for treatment. The chair should offer adequate back and knee support, be a suitable height for the workstation and be comfortable. Ineffective positioning of the client can cause the therapist discomfort, and possibly even injury due to strain. Your elbows should be able to rest on the workstation without stretching. If the client is wearing long sleeves these must be turned up past the elbow to prevent soiling the clothes with the massage product during the treatment. A clean tissue may also be folded along the edge of the sleeve for further protection.

2 Carry out a client consultation, assess the client's needs using different techniques including questioning and natural observation. Complete the client record card, listing all details to ensure the client's suitability for treatment.

3 If the client is wearing nail polish this must be removed to assess the client's nail condition. Use the following procedure:

   a Cleanse the hands with an antiseptic applied with clean cotton wool or a spray to remove surface dirt and micro-organisms.

   b Soak a clean piece of cotton wool in nail polish remover. Place over the nail plate and rest for 2–3 seconds to allow the nail polish to begin to dissolve. Apply firm strokes using the cotton wool over the nail plate surface to remove the polish. Any remaining nail polish left around the cuticle area should be removed using an orange stick tipped with cotton wool. Dip the cotton wool in nail polish remover and remove any remaining nail polish.

> **TIP**
>
> **Work area**
> The work area should be left ready for the next client whenever a treatment is completed.
> Waste products should be disposed of correctly following local council waste disposal regulations.
> If you are free, help other colleagues to tidy the area after treatment to maintain the work area in readiness for the next client.

Removing nail polish to assess the client's nail condition

Workstation set up for manicure

> **TIP**
>
> **Dark nail polish**
> When removing dark nail polish from the nail it might be necessary to replace the cotton wool soaked with nail polish regularly. This is because dark nail polish tends to stain the nails and surrounding skin on removal.

TIP

Treatment sales opportunities
If a nail is split, a nail wrap might be used to strengthen the nail. This should be performed by a senior therapist.

4 Assess the condition of the nails and skin:

a cuticles – are they dry, tight or cracked, or are they soft and supple?

b nails – are they strong, weak, brittle or flaking? Are they discoloured or stained? What shape are they – square, round, oval, long, short, bitten?

c hands – is the skin dry, rough or chapped, or is it soft and smooth?

5 Check with the senior therapist that they agree your nail treatment plan for the client.

6 Confirm and agree with the client the treatment aim and the client's choice of nail finish. Check that the preparation for nail treatment meets the senior therapist's approval.

7 Ask the client to remove jewellery from the treatment area, to prevent it becoming soiled by the massage cream/lotion. Place the jewellery in full view of the client, usually in a tissue-lined bowl or ask the client to look after it for safe keepng passing the jewellery to them. Follow your salon policy.

ACTIVITY

Communication is important with your client
Communication includes talking with your client (verbal communication) and also what your body language is telling the client (non-verbal communication).
You might have given a client a great basic nail treatment but will you be asked to do it again if you are not bright, cheerful and helpful?
Think of three examples of communication used during a basic manicure treatment to gain information about your client and find out if they are happy with the treatment being performed.

EzFlow

Communication involves body language too. What does yours say?

BASIC NAIL TREATMENT PROCEDURE

Outcome 2: Carry out nail treatments

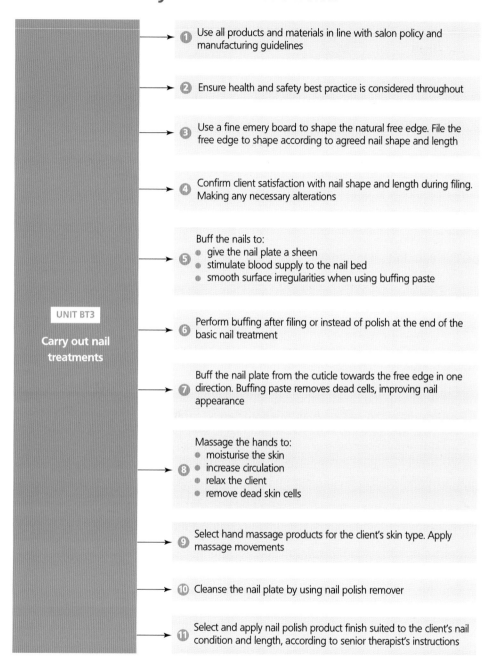

UNIT BT3

Carry out nail treatments

1 Use all products and materials in line with salon policy and manufacturing guidelines

2 Ensure health and safety best practice is considered throughout

3 Use a fine emery board to shape the natural free edge. File the free edge to shape according to agreed nail shape and length

4 Confirm client satisfaction with nail shape and length during filing. Making any necessary alterations

5 Buff the nails to:
- give the nail plate a sheen
- stimulate blood supply to the nail bed
- smooth surface irregularities when using buffing paste

6 Perform buffing after filing or instead of polish at the end of the basic nail treatment

7 Buff the nail plate from the cuticle towards the free edge in one direction. Buffing paste removes dead cells, improving nail appearance

8 Massage the hands to:
- moisturise the skin
- increase circulation
- relax the client
- remove dead skin cells

9 Select hand massage products for the client's skin type. Apply massage movements

10 Cleanse the nail plate by using nail polish remover

11 Select and apply nail polish product finish suited to the client's nail condition and length, according to senior therapist's instructions

Step-By-Step: Basic nail-treatment procedure

1 Cleanse the client's hands with an antiseptic applied with clean cotton wool or a spray to remove surface dirt and micro-organisms. If the nails are dirty it might be necessary to soak them in warm water with a mild detergent before treatment. An orange stick tipped in cotton wool can then be used to gently clean under the free edge of the nail; care should be taken when doing this.

2 File the nails into the agreed shape and length; the part of the nail that is filed is the free edge. Use the lighter, fine textured side of the emery board when filing the nails into shape. The darker, coarser textured side of the emery board is used to remove length. File the nails from side to centre when creating an oval or round shape, with the emery board angled slightly under the free edge. To achieve a square shape, file straight across the top of the free edge in swift, strokes and gently curve the edges. File the nail length so that they are even in shape and length. Run your finger along the edge of the free edge to ensure they are smooth; any roughness should be removed using the fine side of the emery board in an upwards stroke. This is known as bevelling.

3 Buff the nails. Buffing is used to:
   - give the nail plate a sheen
   - stimulate blood supply to increase nourishment to the nail to improve the strength and health of the nail
   - smooth surface irregularities on the nail plate, such as ridges.

   Buffing is carried out after filing; it can also be used in preference to nail polish application, as in the case of a male nail treatment. If it is being used, buffing paste is applied: take a small amount from the container with a clean orange stick and apply this to each nail plate. With the fingertip, use downward strokes from the cuticle to the free edge to spread the paste over the nail plate, avoiding contact with the cuticle. Hold the buffer loosely in your hand, buff in one direction only from the cuticle towards the free edge. Approximately six strokes are applied to each nail plate.

HEALTH AND SAFETY ✚

Filing the nails

Never file completely down the sides of the nails, as strength is required here to prevent breakage. Allow about 4 mm of nail growth to remain at the sides of the nail to provide strength.

TIP ✓

Filing the nails to suit the client's hands and nails

When filing the nails, ensure that the finished appearance suits the client's nail/hand.
If their fingers are **long** and **thin**, select a rounded/square shape and keep the nail length short.
If their fingers are **short** and **fat**, the nails should be filed into an oval shape and the nail length should be longer to make the fingers appear longer and slimmer.

TIP ✓

Cutting the nails

It might be more practical to reduce nail length by cutting the nail at the free edge with nail scissors. These must be sterilised before use.
Support the nail at the sides with one hand of the free edge being cut. This minimises client discomfort. Dispose of the trimmed nail plate hygienically.

4 Apply hand massage after buffing. Massage is applied to:
- moisturise the skin with hand cream
- improve blood circulation and nutrition to the skin and nails
- relax the client
- remove dead skin cells and improve the appearance of the skin.

Select and apply the chosen hand cream/lotion for the client's skin type: dry skin or a male client with coarse body hair will benefit from an oil; normal skin will benefit from a lotion. Use the following procedure:

a Apply using long sweeping strokes from the client's hand to elbow, to both the inner and outer side of the forearm. Repeat 5 times.

b Using the same movements as in step b, using the thumbs, one in front of the other move backwards and forwards over the palm and inner forearm.

c Supporting the finger at the knuckle with one hand, hold the fingers individually and rotate the fingers clockwise and anti-clockwise. Repeat twice.

d Support the client's wrist with one hand and put your fingers between the client's fingers, grasping the hand. Circle the wrist clockwise and then anticlockwise. Repeat twice.

e Repeat step a 5 times.

5 Remove excess oil from the hand cream/lotion. Soak a cotton pad in nail polish remover. The client might find it convenient to put her jewellery back on and pay for her treatment at this stage of the nail treatment to avoid damage to the nail polish after application.

> **TIP** ✓
>
> **Maintaining the quality of the nail polish**
> Clean the neck of the nail polish bottle after use to make sure that it is clean. This will ensure that the seal at the neck of the bottle is tight on closing, preventing the nail polish becoming thick.
>
> Regularly clean the neck of the bottle with cotton wool and nail polish remover.
>
> A product called solvent can be added to restore consistency to thick nail polish. Use according to manufacturer's instructions.

TIP ✓

Too much polish

Avoid having too much polish on the brush during nail polish application.

A thick application of polish will increase the time the nail polish takes to dry and could cause it to run onto the surrounding skin. Two thin coats are better than one thick coat.

6 Nail polish application: nail polish is applied to coat the nail plate for the following reasons:

- for cosmetic improvement to the nail's appearance
- to disguise stained nails
- to add strength to weak nails
- as a specialist nail treatment, e.g. nail strengthener and ridge filler polish.

Use the following procedure:

a Remove excess grease remaining on the nail plate following the massage by applying nail polish remover to the nail plate surface with clean cotton wool. This will help the nail polish stick to the nail plate.

b Check that the edge of the nail is still smooth and even, refile as necessary.

c Select and apply nail polish according to manufacturer's instructions. The correct nail polish application technique is shown below.

d Select a base coat or nail strengthener polish to suit the nail condition.

e Unscrew the bottle top to which the brush is attached. Wipe the brush on one side against the neck of the bottle, turn the brush around and apply the side of the brush with polish to the nail.

f Start with the thumb, apply three brush strokes down the length of the nail towards the cuticle, but avoid contact with the cuticle. The first stroke is down the centre of the nail and then down each side.

g Apply one coat.

h If polish comes into contact with the skin, remove with an orange stick tipped in clean cotton wool and dampened with nail polish remover.

TIP ✓

Fast drying spray

A fast-drying spray product can be applied to reduce the drying time of the polish

Correct polish application

If agreed, apply coloured polish in the same way:

a Apply two coats of a cream polish and three coats if pearlised (frosted).

b A light, neutral colour is suited to short nails. Stronger, darker colours are suited to healthy longer nails and if a dramatic effect is required.

c Apply a top coat. If using a pearlised polish, a top coat is not applied.

d Check the result meets with client and senior therapist satisfaction.

Practise your nail treatment until you can complete it in the allocated time. This is important to ensure the treatment is cost effective and clients are not delayed.

ACTIVITY

Client dissatisfaction with the treatment

Examples of reasons why clients may not be happy with the treatment they have received include:

● the treatment start time was delayed
● the treatment was rushed
● poor therapist communication skills: good communication skills helps the client to relax and enjoy their treatment and feel confident to ask you questions about their treatment
● poor hygiene practice.

Can you add further reasons to the list why a client may not be happy with their treatment? Remember, an unhappy client may not return to the salon!

COMPLETING NAIL TREATMENTS

Outcome 3: Complete the treatment

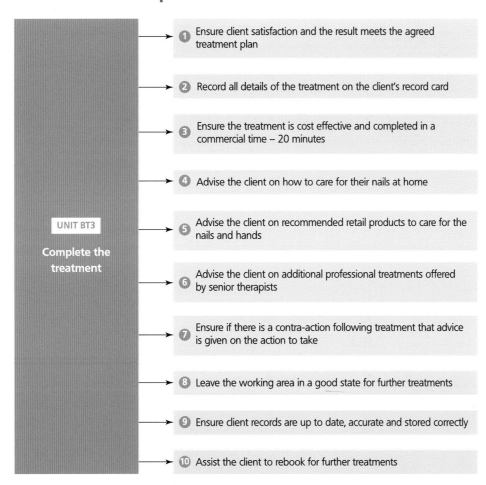

UNIT BT3

Complete the treatment

1 Ensure client satisfaction and the result meets the agreed treatment plan

2 Record all details of the treatment on the client's record card

3 Ensure the treatment is cost effective and completed in a commercial time – 20 minutes

4 Advise the client on how to care for their nails at home

5 Advise the client on recommended retail products to care for the nails and hands

6 Advise the client on additional professional treatments offered by senior therapists

7 Ensure if there is a contra-action following treatment that advice is given on the action to take

8 Leave the working area in a good state for further treatments

9 Ensure client records are up to date, accurate and stored correctly

10 Assist the client to rebook for further treatments

TIP

Maintaining the working area
It is important that you work in a hygienic, organised manner and that you leave the workstation neat and tidy, with all waste materials removed both during and at the end of the treatment.

ACTIVITY

Design an aftercare leaflet
Design an aftercare leaflet for your client that they can read to learn how they should look after and care for their nails/hands at home.

At the end of treatment, make sure the client records are up to date. This is important because you will need to refer to them in the future. The record card should then be stored securely.

The client should be given homecare advice on how to care for the nails at home. This will differ for each client, depending on individual needs.

Basic homecare and advice

- Wear protective rubber gloves when washing up.
- Wear protective gloves when gardening or doing housework.
- Dry the hands thoroughly after washing.
- Apply hand cream regularly to moisturise the skin of the hands and nails.
- Avoid harsh, drying soaps.
- Do not use the fingernails as tools, this causes the nails to weaken and split and break.

Advise the client that the interval between nail treatments is usually 7–10 days.

Advise the client on a treatment plan to improve the nail/skin condition as necessary, and what other professional treatments you could recommend within your responsibility.

Promoting products

Providing advice also gives you the opportunity to recommend retail products, such as nail strengthener and hand cream. This enhances the salon's retail sales and profit.

Contra-actions

Ask clients to contact the salon immediately and speak with the senior therapist if any unwanted reaction to the treatment occurs. Such *contra-actions* (e.g. an allergy, recognised by redness, swelling and inflammation) should be noted on the client's record for future reference.

Ensure the client's treatment card is completed accurately with all details of the treatment recorded. Store the record card securely in compliance with the Data Protection Act 1998.

TIP

Gloves
Gloves provide a barrier to protect the hands and nails from chemical detergents that could cause the skin and nails to become dry and chapped. They also prevent the nails from becoming dry causing peeling and breaking.

Glossary

Base coat	a nail polish product applied to protect the natural nail and prevent staining from coloured nail polish
Bevelling	a nail filing technique used at the free edge of the nail to ensure that it is smooth
Buffer	a nail tool used to improve the appearance of the nail plate and stimulate blood to the nail bed area
Buffing paste	a coarse cream with a gritty texture; it removes surface cells from the nail plate
Consultation	Assessment of a client's needs using different assessment techniques, including questioning and natural observation
Contra-action	an unwanted reaction to the treatment occurring during or after the treatment
Contraindication	a reason or condition that prevents or restricts you from performing a treatment
Cuticle	the part of the skin found around the base of the nail
Data Protection Act (1998)	legislation designed to protect client privacy and confidentiality
Emery board	a nail file used to shape the free edge of the nail
Free edge	the part of the nail that grows beyond the end of the finger
Hand cream/oil	a cosmetic mixture of waxes and oils applied to soften the skin of the hands and cuticles
Massage	movements applied to the skin using the hands to improve its condition and functioning
Matrix	the growing area of the nail, found at the bottom of the nail
Nail	protective, hard shield found at the end of the fingers
Nail bed	the part of the skin covered by the nail plate
Nail plate	the part of the nail the covers the nail bed, the part of the skin upon which the nail plate rests.
Nail polish	a clear or coloured nail product that adds colour/protection to the nail
Nail strengthener	a nail polish product that strengthens the nail plate, which has a tendency to split.
Orange stick	a disposable wooden tool for use around the cuticle and free edge of the nail
Scissors	nail tools used to shorten the length of the nail before filing
Top coat	a nail polish product applied over another nail polish to provide additional strength and durability to the finish

Assessment of knowledge and understanding

Unit BT3: Assist with nail treatments on the hands

You have now learnt how to perform a basic nail treatment to improve the appearance and condition of the hands, nails and surrounding skin. The skills developed enable you to professionally assist with nail treatments on the hands.

To test your level of knowledge and understanding, answer the following short questions, these will prepare you for your summative (final) assessment.

Anatomy and physiology

1 Draw a cross-section of the nail to show the parts:

    a matrix
    b cuticle
    c free-edge
    d nail plate
    e nail bed.

2 Briefly describe the function of each part of the nail listed above.

3 Name the four different nail shapes shown:

Prepare for nail treatments

1 Name ten items required when setting up the work area for a basic nail treatment and explain the purpose of each.

2 Why is it important that existing nail polish is removed before treatment starts?

3 Why is it important that you wash your hands thoroughly before treatment starts? Give two reasons why.

4 Why must accurate up to date records of the client's treatment be kept?

5 Why is it important to follow the senior therapist's instructions for treatment application?

6 What is the purpose of the client consultation?

7 Why is it important to talk to your client during the treatment?

8 Name three contra-indications to basic nail treatment.

Carry out nail treatments

1 How does buffing improve the appearance of the nails?

2 Which side of the emery board is used to reduce the length of the nails?

3 How is a square nail shape achieved when filing?

4 When would you select to use a nail strengthener?

5 State three effects of massage used in a nail treatment on the hands.

Assessment of knowledge and understanding

6 What is the purpose of:

   a base coat

   b top coat

7 State two effects that could be caused by incorrect technique when filing.

8 How should you position yourself when performing basic nail treatment? Why is your working position important?

Complete the nail treatment

1 Why is it important to complete the nail treatment in the given time?

2 State three pieces of home-care advice that could be given to a client

3 Where should a client's records cards be stored on completion of treatment?

4 What retail product could you recommend to a client?

5 What advice would you give a client about contra-actions to treatment?

index

COLEG GLAN HAFREN LRC PARADE